V. V. KOZLOV

THE RUSSIAN MENTALITY

as a Fundamental Factor
in Russian Management Methods

How a society with such a mentality can achieve
success in the modern world

London. 2022

Hertfordshire Press Ltd © 2022
e-mail: publisher@hertfordshirepress.com
www.hertfordshirepress.com

THE RUSSIAN MENTALITY
AS A FUNDAMENTAL FACTOR
IN RUSSIAN MANAGEMENT METHODS

KOZLOV V. V.

English

Second Edition

English Language Editor: Stephen M. Bland
Typeset& cover: Alexandra Rey

All rights reserved. No part of this book may be reprinted or reproduced or utilised in any form or by any electronic, mechanical, or other means, now known or hereafter invented, including photocopying and recording, or in any information storage or retrieval system, without permission in writing from the publishers.

British Library Catalogue in Publication Data
A catalogue record for this book is available from the British Library
Library of Congress in Publication Data
A catalogue record for this book has been requested

ISBN: 978-1-913356-48-4

TABLE OF CONTENTS

INTRODUCTION	7
PREFACE TO THE SECOND EDITION	8
WHAT IS MENTALITY?	17
THE RUSSIAN MENTALITY IN THE VIEW OF RUSSIAN THINKERS ABROAD	22
THE BASIC CONDITIONS FOR THE FORMATION OF RUSSIAN AND WESTERN EUROPEAN MENTALITIES AND THE FUNDAMENTAL DIFFERENCES BETWEEN THEM	33
CHANGES IN MENTALITY BROUGHT ABOUT BY EXTERNAL FACTORS IN A RAPIDLY CHANGING WORLD	39
THE MENTALITIES OF VARIOUS COUNTRIES AND PEOPLES The Differences in Mentalities of Various Countries and Peoples The Differences in the Mentalities of Various Countries and Peoples (continued, values)	46
GENETIC, CULTURAL CODE, ARCHETYPES	65
LAW AND JUSTICE	71
RUSSIAN MANAGEMENT	78
FREEDOM OF THE PRESS	87
RUSSOPHOBIA AND NATIONALOPHOBIA External and Internal Russophobia… The Emergence and Development of Nationalophobia	93

PROBLEMS HINDERING THE RUSSIAN ECONOMY FROM OCCUPYING A WORTHY PLACE IN THE WORLD: CORRUPTION, BUREAUCRACY, NEPOTISM, AS A PERSONNEL POLICY *111*
Corruption
Bureaucracy

NEPOTISM AS A PERSONNEL POLICY *117*
THE UNDERDEVELOPMENT OF CIVIL SOCIETY

127
CONCLUSION

134
SELECTED BIBLIOGRAPHY

136
REVIEW

ABOUT THE AUTHOR

V.V. Kozlov, Doctor of Economics, Professor. Member of the Dissertation Council of the Russian University the name of Plekhanov, author of about 50 scientific works, including monographs, articles, textbooks and teaching aids. He is a veteran of nuclear energy of Russia. From 1990 to 1998, he headed the company- "Atomenergoexport", in 1998–2003- General Director of the company- "Atomstroyexport." Since 2005 professor of the Russian Economic Academy G.V. Plekhanov.

FROM THE AUTHOR

I would like to express my sincere gratitude to Mikhail Nikolaevich Kulapov, who during the course of my work on this book made a number of valuable suggestions aimed at elucidating the research topic to its fullest potential.

Many thanks to my daughter, Tatyana Kozlova, who, having taken a fresh look at the working text from an unbiased perspective, also made some interesting suggestions which were taken into account in the final version.

THE RUSSIAN MENTALITY

INTRODUCTION

At some point, we have all probably asked ourselves the following questions: who are we, where do we come from, and where are we going? What motivates our actions? What is unacceptable to us; what are we comfortable with, and why? What do we value most in this life?

In many ways, the answers to these questions will make it possible for us to look back over our history and trace the process of the formation of national character, otherwise known as mentality.

A person's mentality determines their attitude to family, friends, society and the state, as well as other peoples and nationalities. It also plays a decisive role in defining the position and role of the state and the way in which those who possess a certain mentality live in the modern world.

The purpose of this study is not to assess the quality of the Russian mentality, whether it is positive or not. This is pointless, since there are no criteria for such an assessment, and almost every nation or people may consider itself worthy of emulation. The Russian mentality is what it is.

The purpose of this study is to analyse how this mentality was formed, based on the evidence of scientists, philosophers, publicists, and contemporaries from previous eras. To this end, it is important to attempt to define its specific features in comparison with the mentalities of other peoples, and to determine what needs to be done in order for a society with such a mentality to achieve success in the modern world.

PREFACE TO THE SECOND EDITION

This book was written, and its first edition was published, at a time of relative global political stability. At this time the Covid-19 pandemic had just begun, bringing with it a global economic downturn and exacerbating all contradictions. The situation in Europe and worldwide seemed favourable for further networking, expanding cultural ties, and finding ways to improve mutual understanding between Europeans and Russians. That was the goal I was trying to achieve by taking on the task of writing this book.

When this book was first published, the possibility of a Russian military operation in Ukraine was not seriously considered by the United States, Russia or the European Union. At least that is how it seemed to the average person. Although military conflicts in the Middle East, in which Russia and the West supported opposing sides, were a reality, no one could imagine that the crisis between the collective West and Russia would come to a head in a military operation in the heart of Europe, in Ukraine.

At the same time, however, there was already a sense that a serious conflict was brewing between the West and Russia. Undoubtedly, there are fundamental economic and political differences at the root of the conflict, but I did not consider them when writing this book. My main focus was the difference between the Western and Russian mentalities, and the historical roots that have shaped the Russian mentality. I saw my task as searching for the causes of misunderstanding between them, assuming that an awareness of the differences in mentality, and a possible view of the situation from the opponent's perspective, would help to mitigate the crisis in the relationship, at least on a human level. Time has shown that

THE RUSSIAN MENTALITY

all my fears about the West's misunderstanding - or non-acceptance - of the Russian mentality were by no means unfounded.

In my view, one of the main reasons for the current situation is precisely the lack of understanding of the Russian mentality by Western leaders, both in determining the causes of the crisis in relations, and in formulating the packages of sanctions to be imposed on Russia. In the statements of European Union leaders, for example, there is surprise and bewilderment over the fact that Russia "refuses the prosperity" offered to it by the West. The fact that such "prosperity" is achieved by losing its national sovereignty, and being completely embedded in a system of rules which the West has designed for itself, is kept in brackets; but it is well understood by the Russian population, which does not want to follow this path to "prosperity" at all. The West, not understanding the underlying causes, seems to sense this, so it imposes sanctions not only on Russia as a state, but on all of its people, its culture, science and sport.

As a result, the sanctions are by no means limited to expelling Russia from the economic and financial systems engineered by the West. It has been deemed necessary to expel everything associated with Russia from its humanitarian fields as well, such as the classics of Russian literature and music, previously so valued by Western intellectuals and music lovers. In a number of European countries, productions based on works by Russian writers and on music by Russian composers have been withdrawn, and the contracts of conductors, musicians and singers have been terminated.

Russian athletes have been banned from international competitions and excluded from world federations, at the behest of Western countries. After a series of persecutions and scandals, the exclusion of the Russian team from the Beijing Paralympics looks morally indefensible. There has also been an attack on Russian science. This did not stop at cancelling previously allocated grants: the West moved to expel Russian professors from the academic boards of foreign universities.

Domestic Russophobia has also begun to grow. This is particularly difficult for citizens of Russia living outside the country. Although the leaders of many countries make statements about the inadmissibility of racially motivated hatred, the general atmosphere of persecution of all Russians makes their lives abroad difficult.

The apotheosis of the nationalist approach to the Russian issue has been the authorisation by the Meta corporation to publish posts calling for "Kill the Russians". The fact that such appeals can only be posted by citizens of the former Soviet space and Eastern European countries, and only in the context of events in Ukraine, in no way limits the devastating effects of this decision. In my view, it has become an effective way of fomenting Russophobia on the Internet.

Western countries are trying to hit all groups and strata of the Russian population with their sanctions. Russian oligarchs, even those who have always tried to stay out of politics and contribute in countries where their capitals have found refuge, are losing money, yachts and real estate. The sacred Western right of inviolability of property does not apply to them, because they are Russians. In their new role as victims for the motherland, they even find a certain sympathy among their fellow countrymen.

For ordinary citizens, there is punishment in the form of restrictions on travel to Europe, which is achieved by prohibiting visas and cancelling air travel. Those who can only experience the western way of life in Russia are to be punished by being denied access to western culture in the form of American films, and from the western way of life in the form of fast food chains. All these measures should plant fear, remorse, and an irresistible desire to overthrow their government in the people of Russia.

As a result of the measures taken, we see how ignoring the emotional aspect can lead to the opposite results. As a result of the special operation in Ukraine and all the sanctions imposed, the approval rating of the Russian president has risen to above 70 per cent. Different polls estimate an

THE RUSSIAN MENTALITY

increase of between 4 and 10 percent. Russian society is consolidating. I think that the main factor that led to this result is the total aversion of the Russian population to external pressure, forcing people to rally around the government to defend the state and its sovereignty.

On the material side, Western sanctions will lead to an imminent fall in living standards in Russia. But this is a double-edged sword, as residents of the United States, and especially Europe, will face economic problems as well. Of course economic factors will play a very significant role, maybe a determining one. But there is another factor, which I would describe as a "clash of mentalities". In the end, the chances of emerging from the current situation are higher for those who believe they are right, and are prepared to face possible difficulties.

It is difficult to predict how resilient the behaviour of the modern Russian will be to the material factor. Nevertheless, there is a high probability that the level of resistance of Russians to falling living standards is higher than that of Europeans or Americans. Russia's older generations received a kind of inoculation when they faced impoverishment and lawlessness during the crisis of the 90s, when it was very easy for the country to slide into chaos. Of course all sorts of things happened then, but the majority of people got through this difficult period with dignity, perhaps because the material factor for the Russian person is not the 'be all and end all', as I wrote about in this book. I want to believe that the population of the Western countries also has a certain level of resistance to a reduction of living standards, otherwise this whole process can end in chaos, which is contrary to the interests of mankind.

In conclusion, I would like to express my regret and disappointment that instead of rapprochement and cooperation, which my book was intended to support, Russia and the West have entered a phase of confrontation. Nevertheless, let me express the hope that this period will end sooner rather than later, and that we will once again live in a world that takes into account and respects the interests and specifics of each nation, including its national mentality.

AFTERWORD

As noted in the previous chapter, a fundamental feature of the period under review is the structural transformation of the world economy.

It could be assumed that in the current situation, the destruction of the existing world order of liberal globalisation in the interests of the USA will be accompanied by the formation of a new world economic order, the development of which will take place in the competition of integration structures with centres in China and India, while the EU, the USA and, hopefully, the "Euro-Asian Economic Community" will retain a significant influence.

The emerging new world economic order also has several possible options.

The first one has already been formed in China. It is characterized by a combination of institutions of state planning and market self-organization, state control over the main parameters of economic reproduction and free enterprise, the ideology of the common good and private initiative, and demonstrates a stunning effectiveness in the management of economic development. This has been evident in the manifold growth rates of the advanced industrial sectors over the past three decades, and has been reiterated by performance indicators even during the pandemic.

The second type of integrated world economy is taking shape in India, which is the largest real functioning democracy in the world. The foundations of the Indian system were laid by Mahatma Gandhi and

Jawaharlal Nehru. Their correctly chosen priorities boosted the key areas of the new technological paradigm, and today India is the global number one in terms of economic growth.

The third variant of the new world economic order can be discerned in the mirage of a growing pandemic of mass psychosis. Bids for the formation of a new world order are being initiated from the bowels of the deep state of the USA. On the wave of the pandemic, institutions that purport to govern humanity are being created. In other words, the third variety of the new world order involves, in fact, the formation of a world government led by the American ruling elite in the interests of finance capital, which controls the emission of world currency, transnational banks and corporations, and the global financial market. It is a continuation of the trend of liberal globalisation, augmented by authoritarian technologies to control the populations of countries deprived of national sovereignty.

The current world events show that the US leaders have bet on the third kind of formation of the new world economic order, which has already led the world into a state of extreme turbulence.

The transition from competition to active confrontation between the leading world powers in the struggle for the redistribution of spheres of influence in the world has begun!

PREFACE

In recent years, the category of mentality has been widely used to explore various aspects of socio-economic processes, including management issues. Mentality as a set of features, attitudes and orientations of specific social groups has attracted a great deal of research. Meanwhile, the influence of the Russian mentality on the development of post-Soviet Russia has remained largely neglected as a subject in the published works of modern Russian authors. Moreover, various pro-government business leaders have repeatedly attempted to launch almost explicit campaigns to "re-work" the traditional foundations of national consciousness and mentality formation. The strategies employed involve taking over and "messing" with the minds of the Russian youth by means of mass culture, destroying traditional communication skills, initiatives to suppress the trend of continuous literacy, and eradicating the outstanding achievements of Soviet-era high schools.

In relation to national values, mentality as a process of forming a set of specific cultural and ethnic features is that unique quality which endows the peoples of our planet with their own unique traditions, customs and attitudes. Much of this work is devoted to exploring the birth process of the Russian mentality (particularly as highlighted by the diametrically opposed Western European mentality), including as an integral part of national cultures (with reference to the publications of Russian and foreign philosophers and authors), which was formed and transformed during the development of the Russian State over the course of more than one and a half millennia.

At the same time, the monograph focuses on how the Russian mentality has influenced the development of modern Russian society, including the issues of management and governance, legal nihilism, various types of rights and freedoms, corruption in power structures and among regional leaders, personnel policy, and Russia's place in the escalating contradictions of a rapidly developing world.

In my view, the author's research sheds light on the role of mentality as a fundamental factor in both Russian and foreign management models, offering a valuable interpretation of the matter. This is precisely why one of the secondary goals of this study is to determine the reasons for the centuries-old systemic rejection of our people and our state by Western "civilisation," and the thinly veiled consumerist attitude of the leaders and peoples of the Eastern "civilisations." One need only recall the deeply sad and thoughtful words about Russia's friends laid out in the will of Alexander III, the greatest of Russian rulers, for confirmation of this.

An attempt to understand these complexities is in itself a worthy endeavour. Although some of the author's arguments and conclusions are undeniably unconventional and therefore subject to dispute, debate and discussion, this does not reduce the merits of the work and the significance of this research.

Prof. Kulapov M. N.,
Head of the Scientific School
"Theory and Technology of Management"
Plekhanov Russian University of Economics

THE RUSSIAN MENTALITY

WHAT IS MENTALITY?

MENTALITY: a stable orientation of the inner world of a group of people, uniting them into social and historical communities; a set of attitudes and predispositions of people to a certain way of thinking and acting. On the one hand, mentality is a result of culture and traditions; on the other, it is itself a deep source for cultural development. The destruction of mentality can lead to psychological crises and behavioural deviations.[1]

Mentality (lat. mens, mentis — soul, spirit, mind, and alis — others) — a mindset and way of thinking, a set of intellectual, emotional, and cultural features of a worldview and world perception, a set of values inherent to a social or ethnic group, a nation, a social group, or an individual.[2]

The basis (or foundation) of an individual's, nation's or people's mentality is formed over centuries; it changes, however, only in parts, and never affects the structure as a whole, but only the superstructure which was formed over a shorter time under the influence of external circumstances in a rapidly changing world.

Who and what is a 'Russian,' and have they any special qualities distinguishing them from a 'non-Russian'? Let's formalise the question by defining the basic concept more clearly. First of all, is 'Russian' a national or state-territorial concept? Since our goal is to find more or less fundamental distinctive qualities, we naturally ask ourselves: can these differences be significant enough, for example, to delineate between a Russian (by nationality) and a Tatar, who were born in the same country, live on the same street, and were raised in qualitatively similar socio-cultural conditions? If they can, then these are not social, but rather national

---

1 G. Kodzhaspirova, A. Kodzhaspirov, Pedagogical Dictionary, Moscow: "Academy" Publishing Centre, 2001.
2 URL: http://chtooznachaet.ru/mentalitet.html

and racial differences, and are therefore not relevant to the subject of our study. Thus, in our study we define 'Russian' as a state-territorial concept.

By definition in this study a Russian is a person living in Russian society, who was formed under the influence of Russian national culture, its spiritual values and traditions, considers Russian to be their main language of communication, and regards themselves as and identifies with this type of person. 'Russian' is a generalised and abstract concept, as it reflects the qualities of a Russian person living in various historical epochs and representing different social strata of the population. This concept reveals, first and foremost, the typical, general characteristics of a Russian person. These include, firstly, a kind of unique combination of positive and negative qualities; secondly, contradiction and complexity; and thirdly, high potential and a demand for these basic qualities in modern society.

The Russian mentality as an integral part of national culture is determined by a combination of characteristics. A general overview of the opinions of many researchers makes it possible to identify various qualities of the 'Russian character' as they are reflected in the works of Russian classical literature, historical and philosophical studies (N. Berdyaev, S. Bulgakov, I. Goncharov, L. Gumilyov, F. Dostoevsky, I. Ilyin, V. Klyuchevsky, N. Leskov and others). These include being easily led and passive, a contradictory nature (a juxtaposition of the 'angelic and the demonic'), a love of beauty, self-sacrifice and cruelty in love, Russian prowess and a longing for wide open spaces, a disregard of all measure, a simultaneous hunger for freedom and slavery, submission, blind faith in a good king or fate, lack of self-discipline and self-restraint, a fear of and desire for suffering, and a peculiar kind of holiness which unites both religiosity and atheism. We should also mention strong willpower, perseverance, humility, a practical frame of mind, a quick wit and rationality, optimism, a powerful sense of unity with one another, and a tolerance and acceptance of neighbouring peoples.

In their works, the above-mentioned Russian authors have laid out the unique set of features that define a Russian, identified their positive and negative qualities, pointed out their contradictory nature, thereby creating a kind of generalised portrait, and tried to foresee how it would develop. Thus, for instance, N. A. Berdyaev noted that Russians are deeply dependent on the Eurasian essence of Russia, analysed the contradictory nature of this, and presented some possible ways that Russians may evolve in the future.

N. O. Lossky examined the combination of positive and negative qualities in Russians, noting the special importance of such features as religiosity, kindness and spirituality. I. A. Ilyin identified the unique and peculiar ways in which the character of a Russian manifests itself in various specific historical circumstances. D. S. Likhachev underscored the contradictory nature of the main human qualities in Russian society. V. S. Barulin considered the development processes of a Russian person in Soviet society, identifying their unique combination of different and often contradictory qualities, and highlighting their potential for positive development. However, the studies from this time did not pay due attention to other important questions, such as what fundamental qualities have characterised Russians since their initial historical appearance up until the present day, what main qualities characterise Russians in Russian society today, and what are the possible ways in which Russians in Russia may develop in the near future?

It is interesting to approach the issue of mentality by analysing the impact of geographical location, cultural environment and nature. In this respect, such groups of factors as geographical location (vast open spaces), climate (long winters, low temperatures, etc.), and landscape are noteworthy.

The first group of factors determines the following character traits: breadth of the soul, a desire for freedom and spiritual expansion, moodiness, impracticality and poor management skills, lack of initiative, and laziness.

The second produces melancholy, pensiveness, a tendency to underestimate the value of one's work, hospitality, patience, obedience, a group mentality, a sense of collective unity and camaraderie, and a contradictory and unrestrained nature.

The third is conducive to contemplation, dreaminess, observation, thoughtfulness and a tendency to search for meaning in the workings of nature.

The Russian historian, Vasily Osipovich Klyuchevsky, once noted a typical feature of Russians: 'Nowhere else in Europe will we be able to find such a lack of habit to regular, moderate and measured constant work as in great Russia.' The author finds reason for this, however, in Russia's history: 'Russia is a country of risky agriculture, where every third or fifth year the harvests failed. The short agricultural cycle — 4–5 months — forced the farmer to be in a constant hurry. This is precisely why people had to work in emergency mode when it was critical and react to circumstances the rest of the time.'[3]

An important feature of the Russian mentality is dreaminess. Perhaps it is, amongst other reasons, a result of the fact that Tsar Boris Godunov issued an edict in 1592 enslaving peasants. As a consequence, most of our ancestors rarely left their native villages. This injustice, exacerbated by poverty, has led to collective fantasies and dreams of universal justice, wellbeing, beauty and goodness. In general, Russians have tended to live in their dreams of the future. They imagined that the harsh and dull reality of everyday life was merely a bump on the road to another life where everything would be different and where they would find reason, true happiness and joy. The whole meaning of life was in this imagined future, whereas the present counted for nothing.

---

3   Klyuchevsky V. O. The Course of Russian History: in 5 parts. — St. Petersburg, 1904–1922.

At various stages of historical development, all manifestations of folk consciousness reflect this contradictory feature of the national spirit when set against everyday actualities — a readiness for utopia, along with the firm belief that utopia can become a reality.

Of course, the mentality of any nation finds its expression through models of perception and behaviour which affect the political and economic life of the country. Moreover, this mentality is based on historical experiences. Thus, for instance, Russians and Americans may perceive the same event from entirely different perspectives simply because of their different mentalities. Each people will have their own truth and attempting to change the minds of another people will often prove a thankless task.

Studying national mentality is also useful when trying to understand whom you are dealing with, or even whom you may have to fight. The Germans, for example, have always taken a keen interested in Russians. The first detailed description of Russia was made by the German ethnographer, Johann Gottlieb Georgi in 1776. The title of the work speaks for itself, *A Description of All the Peoples that Inhabit the Russian State - Their Way of Life, Religion, Customs, Homes, Clothing and Other Distinctive Features*. 'Nowhere else on Earth is there a state like the Russian state, containing such a broad spectrum of different peoples,' he wrote. 'These are the Russ peoples, with their tribes such as the Lapps, Semoyads, Yukagirs, Chukchi, Yakuts (the list of various nationalities takes up an entire page)... as well as migrants, such as the Indians, Germans, Persians, Armenians, Georgians.'[4]

Later, German Chancellor Otto von Bismarck would write that he considered the Russians (a group which to his mind included the entire population of Russia) a united nation. 'Even the most favourable outcome of the war will never be able to undermine Russia's main source of strength,' he maintained, 'which is based on a population of millions.'⁵ Bismarck is also credited with saying that 'it is not enough to kill a Russian soldier, you must also strike him down.'

However, history failed to instruct even the pragmatic Germans, which is why Germany suffered a crushing defeat in World War II.

THE RUSSIAN MENTALITY IN THE VIEW OF RUSSIAN THINKERS ABROAD

Obviously, not everyone in Russia was thrilled about the Bolsheviks coming to power in October 1917. Many among of the intelligentsia including well-known professors understood that an intense radicalisation of society would inevitably lead to civil war. Naturally, a sense of distrust immediately arose between them and the new government. Criticism of some of the Bolsheviks actions by these professors led to Lenin suggesting that '20-40 professors be dismissed.' However, setting the trend for what would become a Soviet tradition, the plan was eventually exceeded several-fold, and the layoffs were replaced with exile, both internally and externally.

Nikolai Berdyaev, Ivan Ilyin, Semyon Frank and Boris Vysheslavtsev along with 160 other prominent philosophers, historians and economists would be expelled from the Soviet Union on the Oberburgomister Haken, later nicknamed the "Philosopher's ship." Of the foremost philosophers of the time, only Lossky and Bulgakov remained in Russia, though not for long. The first would be sent by the next steamship from St. Petersburg to Stettin, and the second from Sevastopol to Constantinople.

---

5   URL: https://topwar.ru

In addition to philosophers, the country lost the historians, Karsavin and Myakotin. The expulsion of Pitirim Sorokin was a significant loss from the point of view of academic science.

Although he was only 33-years-old at the time, it was impossible not to note his huge scientific potential. Today, many encyclopaedias and reference books credit Sorokin as the founder of modern sociology, never failing to refer to him as an 'American scientist,' and only occasionally specifying his Russian origin.[6]

A separate page on the history of scientific thought regarding ethnic issues is occupied by Russian scientists, philosophers and thinkers who, for various circumstances, found themselves outside of Russia. Far from their homeland and their people, they turned their gaze to Russia and the people who lived there.

It's fitting that we provide some information on the activities of the philosophers - whose statements are repeatedly cited in this study - after their departure from Russia.

After setting sail on September 29th 1922 on the "Philosopher's ship," Nikolai Alexandrovich Berdyaev lived first in Berlin. In 1924, he moved to Paris, living alternately in the city and in nearby Clamart until his death in 1948. Of the books published by Berdyaev whilst in exile, the following titles are especially noteworthy: *The New Middle Ages* (1924), *The Destiny of Man* (1931), *Slavery and Freedom* (1939), *The Russian Idea* (1946), and *The Experience of Eschatological Metaphysics: Creativity and Objectification* (1947). Many other works were published posthumously, including *Self-Knowledge: An Essay in Autobiography*, and *The Realm of Spirit and the Realm of Caesar* (1949). Between 1942 and 1948, Berdyaev was nominated for the Nobel Prize in Literature seven times.[7]

Sergei Nikolaevich Bulgakov was exiled to Constantinople on December 30th 1922. In July 1925, he moved to Paris, where he helped cre-

---

6 Glavatsky M.G. "The Philosopher's Ship":1922: Historiographical studies. Yekaterinburg, 2002.
7 https://ru.wikipedia.org/wiki/Berdyaev,_Nikolai_Alexandrovich#cite_note-16

ate the Orthodox Theological Institute. Bulgakov worked at the institute for the rest of his days, serving as a Professor of the Department of Dogmatic Theology (1925), Inspector (1931), Dean (1940), and Doctor of Church History (1943). He taught courses on Old Testament Scripture and Dogmatic Theology. In late 1927 and early 1928, an Anglo-Russian religious congress was held, resulting in the establishment of the bilateral Commonwealth of Saint Albania and Saint Sergius of Radonezh.[8] In 1934, he took an important trip to the United States which led to an interdenominational initiative involving cooperation with the Anglican Church.

Ivan Alexandrovich Ilyin worked as a professor at the Russian Scientific Institute (RNI) in Berlin from 1923 to 1934. In the 1920s, Ilyin became one of the main ideologists of the Russian White movement in exile, and from 1927 to 1930 he was the editor and publisher of *Russian Bell* magazine. In 1938, he left Germany for Switzerland, where he continued his scientific activities in Zollikon, a suburb of Zurich, until his final days. Here, he wrote the books: *The Singing Heart* and *The Path to Evidence*. Shortly before the end of his life, Ilyin finished and published a manuscript which he had been working for over thirty years — *Axioms of Religious Experience* (1953).[9]

Pitirim Alexandrovich Sorokin met the October Revolution with prejudice. Representing the Socialist Revolutionary Party, he became a member of the Constituent Assembly — the last hope that the country would take a democratic path. Sorokin fought against the Bolsheviks, but became disillusioned with the activities of the Socialist Revolutionaries. In any case, it was no longer possible for a serious sociologist who opposed Lenin to remain in Russia, and in 1922, Sorokin was exiled from the Soviet Union on the "Philosopher's ship." Together with his family,

---

8   *Kozyrev A. P.* BULGAKOV Sergey Nikolaevich // *A. Yu. Andreev, D. A. Tsygankov* Imperial Moscow University: 1755 —1917: encyclopedic dictionary. — M.: Russian Political Encyclopedia (ROSSPEN), 2010. —

9   *Dmitry Butrin*. Philosophical message to the President. *Gazeta.ru* (June 5, 2006).

he settled in the United States, where in 1931 he founded the Sociology Department at Harvard University, which he served as the head of until 1942. He worked as a professor at Harvard until 1959, and in 1965 became President of the American Sociological Association.[10]

The life paths taken by these thinkers and their attitudes to the tragic history of Russia allow us to trust their analysis of the factors forming the basic foundations of the Russian mentality and their key conclusions.

Presented below are quotations from their works which focus on exploring the national mentality, psychology, the causes and consequences of certain forms of behaviour and cultural stereotypes characteristic of Russian people.

EXCERPTS FROM STATEMENTS OF RUSSIAN THINKERS AND PHILOSOPHERS

National character

National character and consciousness are the products of the geographical, political and the socio-economic conditions of people's existence. In the view of N. A. Berdyaev, the more complex and contradictory these conditions, the more complex and contradictory the national character.

Russia is the most 'stateless' and anarchic country in the world, and Russians are the most apolitical of people; they have never been able to organise their homeland, it is absolutely chaotic. The vastness of the Russian terrain has not contributed to the development of self-discipline and initiative in Russians — they dissolve into space.[11]

---

10 (Information source - History portal of the Russian Federation, https://histrf.ru/biblioteka/b/kratkii-kurs-istorii-pitirim-sorokin)
11 Berdyaev N. The Fate of Russia. — M.: EKSMO-PRESS, Kharkiv: Folio, 1999.

Exploring the origins of the formation of the mentality and national spirit, the outstanding theologian and philosopher, S. N. Bulgakov gives precedence to complex ethnographic mixtures. Bulgakov recognises, however, that 'nationalities are born, that is, that there is a historical boundary beyond which the ethnographic mixture transforms into a nation with its own unique being, self-consciousness, instinct, and this nation leads an independent life, fights, defending its existence and identity.'[12]

The famous Russian philosopher, I. A. Ilyin argued that 'contemplation with the heart' was the primary spiritual force of the Russian people. 'The Russian soul,' he noted, 'is first and foremost a child of feeling and contemplation. Its culture-creating act is the essence of heart knowledge and a religiously conscientious impulse. Meanwhile, love and contemplation are free, free as space, as free as the plain, as a living organ of nature, as a praying spirit — this is why the Russian needs freedom, and values it as air for breath, as space for movement. Russian culture is built on feeling and the heart, on contemplation, on freedom of conscience and freedom of prayer. They are the primary forces and attitudes of the Russian soul, which sets the tone for their powerful temperament. The secondary forces are will, conscious thought, legal consciousness, and organisational functions.' Therefore, the Russian people are a people of the heart and conscience. Herein lies their strengths and weaknesses. In contrast to someone from the West, 'everything here is based not on moral reflection, not on "cursed duty and obligation," not on forced discipline or fear of sinfulness, but rather on free kindness and on a somewhat dreamy, sometimes heartfelt contemplation.' To business relations, with their cold, calculating and speculative reason, the Russian contrasts the confidential heart-to-heart conversation in everyday life. Whilst Russians venerate the clever and bow before the strong-willed, above all they love a person of soul, heart, and conscience. To be called a 'soul-person' is

---

12   Bulgakov S. N. Selected / comp., auth. intro. art.: O. K. Ivantsov, PhD.; auth. comments. V. V. Sapov, D. S. Novoselov. — M.: ROSSPEN, 2010.

the highest archetypal praise among Russians. This is why it is so easy for them to turn away from property rights, politics and laws. All of this has no value for the heart; it doesn't bring happiness, peace of mind, or harmony.

Ilyin saw the fundamental contradiction of the Russian national character as its 'fluctuation between weakness of character and the highest heroism.'[13]

The influence of state size on the formation of national character

Broad is the Russian citizen, as broad as the Russian land, as the Russian fields, and Slavic chaos rages within them. The vastness of the terrain has not contributed to the development of self-discipline and initiative in Russians — they dissolve into space, wrote Berdyaev.

Vast spaces were a simple matter for the Russian people, but it was not so easy for them to organise these spaces into the greatest state in the world and to maintain and protect order in it.

State control of Russian spaces was accompanied by a terrible centralisation, the subordination of all life to the state's interest and suppression of personal and social freedoms. Russians have always had a weak sense of personal rights, and class and group initiative was not developed.

The influence of history on the formation of national character

S. N. Bulgakov believed that 'during historical periods when the national consciousness is aroused and sharpened, the eyes and language, lyrics, epics, arts and customs open up.' Pride of place here belongs to

---

13   Ilyin I. A. On the Coming Russia: Selected Articles / Ed. by N. P. Poltoratsky. — M.: Voenizdat, 1993.

language, which captures the soul of the people. It is at once both a 're-flection and creation of the people's soul.'

Berdyaev explains the contradictory psychological makeup of the Russian people by looking to the turbulent and dramatic history of the nation. Changes do not occur at lightning speed; they take place over a significant period. Political and socio-economic disasters to some extent speed up transformative processes.

At the beginning of the century, the Russian mentality underwent a violent break as a result of the 1917 Revolution and the events that followed, which led to the formation of a new Soviet person. As Berdyaev put it: 'The Russian thirst for absolute freedom turned into slavery; the Russian thirst for absolute love turned into hatred.'

Berdyaev believed that the history of the Russian people is one of the most painful. The author cites the struggle against the Tatar invasions and the Tatar yoke, the ever-present hypertrophy of the state, the totalitarian regime of the Muscovy, the Time of Troubles, the split, the violent nature of Peter the Great's reforms, serfdom - which was the most terrible plague on Russian life - the persecution of the intelligentsia, the execution of the Decembrists, and the terrible regime of the Prussian Junkers.

Russia's development was disastrous. The Muscovy period was the worst in Russian history, the most stifling and the most Asiatic-Tatar, and the freedom-loving Slavophiles idealised it purely out of miscomprehension.

The Russians have experienced the ability to inspire intense love or passionate hatred. They are a people whom the West can find very disturbing. Every national identity, like the individuality of a person, is a microcosm, and therefore contains contradictions to varying degrees. In terms of their polarisation and contradictions, the Russian people can only be compared to the Jews, and it is no accident that these peoples have a strong messianic consciousness. The contradictions and complexities of the Russian soul may be due to the fact that the two streams of world history — East and West — collide and interact in Russia. Russians are not a purely European or a purely Asian people. As a place where two worlds meet, Russia is itself two worlds. The Russian soul has always been a battleground between Eastern and Western principles.

It should be noted that Russian thinking has a certain propensity to totalitarian teachings and totalitarian worldviews. That such teachings have found favour here reflects the religious character of the Russian people. The Russian intelligentsia has always sought to develop a totalitarian, holistic worldview in which truth would be united with justice. Through totalitarian thinking, they wanted to create a perfect life, not just perfect works of philosophy, science and art.

The intelligentsia was crushed between two forces — the power of the tsarist government and the power of the people. The intelligentsia perceived the people as a kind of mysterious force. It set itself up in opposition to the people, felt guilty before them, and wanted to serve them. The topic of 'the intelligentsia and the people' is purely Russian, and the West does not understand it.

At the beginning of the century, Russia experienced a cultural Renaissance. Only those who lived through this period understand what a creative upsurge was experienced, and what force of spirit inspired Russian souls. Russia experienced a flowering of poetry and philosophy, intense religious quests, mystical and occult moods. As is the case everywhere, fashion joined the upsurge. Although we experienced a cultural Renaissance, it would be false to say there was a religious Renaissance. There was insufficient strong and focused will for a religious Renaissance; there was too much cultural refinement, and the cultural sphere was defined by a mood of decadence. The Russian soul is characterised by the same boundlessness and striving for infinity as the Russian plain. Therefore, it was difficult for the Russian people to master these vast spaces and give them structure and form.

Patriotism and a sense of homeland as the foundation of the national spirit

According to Ilyin, patriotism and a sense of homeland are the foundation of the national spirit. National character is multifaceted and manifests itself in various ways; however, if these do not grow out of a sense of attachment to the native land it is impossible to talk about the national spirit. A sense of homeland is a 'creative act of spiritual self-determination.' Spiritual culture forms the essence of national consciousness and character. Unlike the peoples of Western Europe, the Russian people were not, for the most part, a people of culture; they were more a people of revelations and inspirations who lacked a sense of good measure and easily fell into extremes.

Formation of the russian state

The Russian people, who for centuries had been expanding their territories, created a country of enormous scale — the Great Russian Empire with its beautiful and unique culture. Painting, literature, architecture, music and cuisine all play a valuable role in forming the culture. Thanks to their worldview and mentality, the Russian people have influenced the world, from Poland to the Pacific Ocean. However, the mentality of a people may undergo a metamorphosis and acquire a new form as a consequence of political and socio-economic realities, and the new form is not always an improvement on the previous one. The ethnic spirit weakens, the morality fades over time, and the people become "Ivans," with no sense of kinship, honour or conscience. This is very dangerous for a nation. Therefore, it is essential to protect one's culture and honour traditions, to know one's history and 'preserve honour from an early age;' hence the indisputable relevance of the topic of the spiritual world for any nation. If we preserve the spiritual world, we will also preserve the material world. The only way a people can continue to bring beauty to the world is by keeping their spiritual world united and sound.

With regard to the Russian nation, however, many people reduce its entire spiritual world to aggression. Liberals in the arts, politics and science focus exclusively on Russian negativity, forgetting altogether the positive side of our people's character. They recall the campaigns in Byzantium and Kazan, Ivan the Terrible, Ermak, the conquest of Siberia, the Caucasus, Central Asia and other territories. Many countries, especially Western ones, accuse us of a multitude of sins where it just so happened that the Slavic breadth of soul called for boundless spaces and unbounded actions. It was drawn to the West and the South, to the North and the East. The freedom-loving tribe hungered for unrestrained freedom, and perhaps this is what carried it to all corners of the globe. The Russians used not only violence and force to advance into foreign lands, however, they also brought enlightenment. They also acquired vast territories in defensive bat tles which turned into justly aggressive ones.[14]

Thus, gradually, over many centuries, in a typically laid back Russian manner, the Russian land was formed with its own unique quirks, traditions, customs, holidays and manners. There were many great victories and many losses as well. Along with the virtuous milestones in Russian history, there are, as with any country, shameful milestones too. There were also discoveries of global importance applauded by millions to this day. All of this is the Russian people. The ambiguous, entirely diverse nature of the Russian nation reflects the vivid diversity of the Russian soul. The Russian nation contains a great wealth of various temperaments and characters. It was formed in severe geopolitical and climatic conditions, in almost continuous military campaigns, in a conservative patriarchal society, in deep religiosity, in the boundless open spaces of its homeland.

When examining this issue, it is necessary to underscore the contributions of the thinker, I. A. Ilyin. In his work, *Our Tasks*, the author aims to strengthen Russian self-awareness, to form a leading national layer in society capable of helping the entire nation realise its creative potential. Ilyin places particular emphasis on the issues of spiritual and moral education, and the formation of legal awareness amongst Russian citizens.

Such thinkers understood that in order to see the inner workings of any person, it is necessary to understand that a person is not only a material substance made up of flesh and blood and driven by physiological needs, but also a spiritual being. Each and every person contains a spiritual world. In one person, this spiritual world may be small, the size of a mere poppy seed, whilst in another it may be so large that those around them will sense it and try to preserve this spiritual legacy for the ages.

---

14   Shchuplenkov O. V. The Russian Person // Philosophical thought. — 2013. — No. 6.

THE BASIC CONDITIONS FOR THE FORMATION OF RUSSIAN AND WESTERN EUROPEAN MENTALITIES AND THE FUNDAMENTAL DIFFERENCES BETWEEN THEM

The fact that the Christian world was at one time almost equally divided between Russia and Europe has given rise to the illusion among some Russian elites that our country is part of a pan-European Christian civilisation. Indeed, the inhabitants of Russia and Western Europe share the same anthropological roots, and most importantly they have always worshipped the same God and been guided by the same Gospel. In other words, the Sermon on the Mount has served to unite the two parts of Greater Europe for the last thousand years.[15]

The difference lies in their perspectives: the Russians considered themselves equal in relations with Europeans, rightly believing the Slavs were just as much at the source of European culture as the Romano-Germans, whilst Western elites never entertained any illusions about a 'single Christian civilisation.' They always regarded Russia, if not as a barbaric and Asian country, European merely by virtue of its geographical location, then at best a backward European relative on the outskirts of the 'civilised' West.

It's worth noting that the Western Christian Church was historically the first global disconnection in relation to original Christianity. Moreover, in contrast to Christ's true followers, who, as we may recall, drove the merchants out of the Temple, the Roman Catholic Church owes its existence to the support of Western Mediterranean merchants. (The Reformation of the Roman Catholic Church in the XVI century followed a similar scheme, when the founder of Protestantism, Martin Luther, was actively supported by the burghers of Germany.) Not only did the Ro-

---

15   The Sermon on the Mount — a collection of sayings by Jesus Christ in the Gospel of Matthew, primarily reflecting the moral teachings of Christ.

man Catholic Church permit merchants into the temple, merchants control the Vatican to this day. The divergent spiritual and moral paths taken by Europe and Russia are the basis of the fundamentally different value systems and, consequently, the modes of behaviour they have formed in the XXI century.

Differences in mentality are likewise a consequence of cultural differences. Cultural attitudes to the concepts of life and death represent a key principle.

In Western Christianity (Catholicism and Protestantism), death is followed by purgatory; therefore, by performing good deeds, salvation and the remission of sins are a possibility. God's Grace manifests itself through one's material prosperity and accumulation of wealth. Conversely, in the Orthodox worldview, wealth was never regarded as a manifestation of Grace, in fact, quite the opposite. Spiritual salvation is achieved by turning away from the material world and distancing oneself from the affairs of society and state.

In Orthodoxy, there is no purgatory; however, preceding the Last Judgment, there are ordeals, which assess the sins one has committed in this Earthly life. In Orthodoxy, one cannot buy one's way out of sin through indulgences as in Catholicism. To be saved, faith alone (as in Protestantism) is not enough, and nor are good deeds (without which faith is dead); above all, one is saved through love.

Whereas Western Christians try to make themselves worthy of God's Kingdom by selfless labour for their own benefit and that of their loved ones, Orthodox Christians 'earn' the right to God's Kingdom not through labour and the accumulation of material wealth, but through self-sacrifice and prayer. For the Orthodox, the main thing in life is not labour, but prayer, grace, and communion with God. In Orthodoxy, labour is merely a constraint necessary to maintain the flesh which houses the spirit. An example of this is St. Seraphim of Sarov, who prayed on a rock in a remote forest for a thousand days and nights.

Above all, it should be noted that Russia began as an agricultural, a productive and creative civilisation which gradually grew through handicrafts and then industrial production. Europe, in contrast, made a leap forward in its development from the moment commercial cities expanded in the Mediterranean and commercial capital formed, which determined the accelerated development of financial capital and its subsequent transformation into industrial capital.

For six centuries, the Russian Empire grew on lands in which mainly farmers and ploughers resided, whereas Europe expanded for four centuries by attaching colonies scattered across all continents by force. Geographical differences and variegated initial economic structures determined the diametric models of behaviour that formed among Russian and European ethnic groups.

The main difference between Russia and Europe involves values, which grow out of a combination of geographical, economic and, consequently, socio-cultural factors; if nomads always followed nature and guarded their right to do so, merchants protected their goods, financiers their capital, and industrialists their assets, then the farmer's way of life is based on protecting their land.

From one age to the next society moves forward, stepping over the 'potholes and pitfalls of history,' including its own mistakes. People think and act based on the information they receive. Before they have information, they think one way, but once they acquire information, they change their minds. Knowledge and development go hand-in-hand with the appearance of certain facts, from living with contemplation to abstract thinking and thence to practise. This is the path to truth.

As a consequence of the Industrial Revolution in the XVII-century in England and Holland, there appeared a philosophy calling on people to hear and respect the opinions of others, even if these opinions differed from theirs. This, in turn, formed the basis of the relationship between the government and the society of that time. In other words, if I'm in power, I will force you to submit to my will on an issue we disagree on, but I won't force you to change your point of view. This kind of culture of relationships subsequently developed and evolved.

Russian culture took a different path. If your views differed from those of the official ideology, it was essential that you publicly repented for your mistakes. Making a public spectacle of repentance is, of course, hypocrisy, but, unfortunately, it satiated society. Under Stalin, it was common practice to renounce parents, husbands and wives, and to renounce one's views if it seemed to satisfy everyone. People would say: 'You see, we've exposed them, and now they've repented.' Everyone would pretend that this was 'Truth' with a capital 'T' — a 'Truth' everyone shared and agreed with.

The situation in Russian society today has changed in that official repression of dissents is now implicit. If you express an opinion that is at odds with certain groups in online social media, you will be eaten alive. In fact, harassment campaigns against dissident thinkers online are, from time to time, organised. Moreover, both groups — pro-government forces and all those in the opposition — employ the same methods.

The agricultural basis of the economy and of Russian life as a whole - even under Catherine the Great, 94% of the population were peasants - determined not only the creative model of Russian behaviour and its non-violent nature, but also a number of other qualities of the mega-ethnic group. These can be defined as: a special attitude to justice (justice is above the law), to the state (the state is not the master, but the supreme judge), to society, family, the individual, etc. A distinctive feature of the Russian soul is unselfishness, because conscience forces you to sacrifice profit.

The pragmatic Western European mentality espouses the golden rule: 'do good to your neighbour, so they will do good to you.' The Western liberal mentality is a system that helps an individual, group, class, or people to adapt to their situation, that is, to the totality of circumstances with all its opportunities and limitations. European culture puts individuality first, viewing it as more valuable than the community and the state; hence the idea of human rights, which are above all else. The Asian influence on the Russian mentality manifests itself in the sense that community is valued above individuality; hence the 'Russian idea' about the necessity of individual self-sacrifice for the sake of the nation's bright future.

Main conclusions on the materials presented in chapters 1 to 4

The main difference between Russia and Europe involves values, which grow out of a combination of geographical, economic and socio-cultural factors.

It should be noted that Russia began as agricultural, that is, a productive and creative civilisation which gradually grew through handicrafts and then industrial production. In contrast, Europe made a leap forward in its development from the moment commercial cities expanded in the Mediterranean and commercial capital formed, which determined the accelerated development of financial capital and its subsequent transformation into industrial capital.

The agricultural mode of the economy and Russian life as a whole determined the creative model of Russian behaviour, its attitude to justice, the state, society, family, and the individual.

In Western Christianity (Catholicism and Protestantism), material prosperity is seen as a manifestation of God's Grace. In the Orthodox worldview, the contrary holds true as salvation is achieved by turning away from the material world.

In Orthodoxy, one cannot buy one's way out of sin as in Catholicism, and neither is faith alone enough as in Protestantism. In Orthodoxy, one is saved through love.

European culture puts individuality first and foremost, viewing it as more valuable than the community and the state. The Asian influence on the Russian mentality manifests itself in the way that community is valued above individuality, hence, the 'Russian idea' about the necessity of individual self-sacrifice for the sake of the nation's future.

CHANGES IN MENTALITY BROUGHT ABOUT BY EXTERNAL FACTORS IN A RAPIDLY CHANGING WORLD

According to many researchers, mentality is a complex phenomenon which develops over many centuries, if not millennia. Some researchers believe that the task of changing mentality is, from the outset, an exercise in futility. However, modern social psychology suggests that mentality is not immutable, noting a correlation between changes in living conditions and social relations and changes in mentality.

Today, no one would seriously claim that our mentality has not changed since the Middle Ages. Therefore, we will not argue that the modern Russian mentality was formed under Peter the Great or in some other bygone age.

In purely practical terms, viewing mentality as immutable often leads to a lack of motivation to change anything for the better, to improve oneself or social relations. Rather, it should be noted that mentality can change reasonably quickly — in two or three decades. South Korea and Singapore are an excellent case in point, as both countries have dramatically changed in the course of a generation.

Let's take a purely Russian example: the reforms of Alexander II which particularly affected the judicial system. As a result, jury trials and many lawyers appeared in Russia. These jurors were ordinary citizens, but, I assure you, despite knowing full well what decisions the authorities wanted, they often returned the opposite verdicts. As a consequence, a completely different attitude to the court developed in the Russian Empire — it was viewed as a just institution in which one could defend one's rights. Before Alexander II, no such attitude to the judicial system existed.

Of course, all people have their own national and ethnic specifics. That notwithstanding, it's hard to ignore the defining role played by our social relations and the social environment in which we live. Changes in the social environment produce changes in mentality.

We tend to assume that from time immemorial in Russia laws have been disregarded, and that is just the way it is, unlike in the West, where almost everyone lives by the letter of the law. According to European and American expats who come to live and work in Moscow, after a short time nearly all of them begin to violate traffic rules and give bribes to the police. One American woman, when asked why she does this, replied that it would never have occurred to her to bribe the police in America, but in Moscow 'there's no other way.'

So, as we can see, the mentality of a particular American can change fundamentally as they adapt to the Russian environment. This same example also suggests something else, though. It has only been fairly recently that Americans and Germans have begun to 'live by the law' en masse — a hundred or so years. We can take the same path and do so much faster.

In the last hundred years — a historically insignificant period of time — Russia has changed three times and has done so qualitatively. It follows that people raised in fundamentally different conditions should be fundamentally different. It is precisely these differences that I would like to identify.

Mentality is transformed due to the fact that both individuals in society and society as a whole undergo changes in consciousness. The evolutionary path of the Russian mentality has been a long one, but although it has undergone significant changes the mental essence has remained unchanged. This is because that mentality was formed under the influence of natural, climatic, religious and geographical factors; factors which laid the groundwork, in the view of Russian social philosophers (Berdyaev,

Ilyin, Lossky) for the formation of the core of the Russian mentality. V. P. Lyubchak points out that the specificity of the Russian mentality is fundamental in its nature.

The second group of factors can be referred to as socio-situational (economic, political and cultural). They presuppose a situational behavioural rationality through awareness of reality, resulting in the formation of values and stereotypes. The socio-situational level of mentality is laid over top of the fundamental basis, and it is this level which is more subject to change.[16]

Since 1917, more than three generations of Russians have come and gone, which has inevitably led to a change to the features that characterised the citizens of pre-revolutionary Russia. Although the present period of development is quite fast-paced, obviously it too is catalysing the formation of new features in the mentality of Russian citizens. Thus, we inevitably focus our attention on those Russian features which were formed from the beginning of the XIX century to the present.

Let's take a look at the most momentous events of this period and consider their influence on the formation of the features in question.

Two centuries ago, political unrest began stirring in Russia, eventually leading to the Revolution of 1917. Thanks to the Decembrists, the rather narrow layer of Russian intelligentsia began regarding the common folk (much like some modern sociologists do) as an amorphous and ignorant mass, which, through the efforts of enlightened minds, must be brought to the light of truth and happiness. Claiming to have the welfare of the common people in mind, the Decembrists categorically did not wish to allow these same people an active role in their political projects. The army, headed by an educated officer, was to take care of all matters. According to the plan of their leader, P. Pestel, the people would have a ten-year transition period in which to slowly adapt to independence,

---

16   Lyubchak V. P. Specifics of the Russian Mentality in the Context of Peacekeeping Issues. GOU VPO "Tomsk State University", 2010.

freedom and the absence of lordly oversight. Meanwhile, the country would be covered with a network of schools, thereby giving people access to education.

If this ambitious plan to remake Russian society had succeeded, we would be living in a different country. However, it didn't work; the Decembrists were exiled to Siberia, and the Russian people remained ignorant of how they were to find happiness in a mere ten to fifteen years.

The state need not be an empire. The state can be a national state, living by its own interests and yet still adhering to an imperial ideology. Under Alexander I, the first half-hearted attempt to transform Russia from a 'country of slaves into a country of citizens' was undertaken. Alexander I nurtured the green shoots of the future civil society, observing the secret societies of the future Decembrists without dispersing them whilst seeing in them a potential future threat. He left behind a state where there could no longer be a place for 'Bironovism'[17] and palace coups. With his death, though, the movement towards civil society in Russia stopped for a long time. There were some objective reasons for this. A terrible external threat in the shape of Napoleon befell Russia, showing both Alexander and Nicholas I, who came to the throne after him, that a strong army was more important for a state than reveries, so to speak, of freedom for a people who were not yet ready for it.

After the Decembrists left the stage, new actors appeared on the Russian political scene — the Narodniks. Unlike the Decembrists, the Narodniks believed that people are responsible for shaping their own fate, and their historical mission was to rock the boat and stir up an explosion of popular indignation. Such an explosion would empower the people to arrange everything by themselves for their own benefit.

That said, it should be noted that for almost the entire XIX century, all attempts to communicate with the people resembled not so much a

---

17   'Bironovism,' or the dominance of foreigners in all areas of state and public life — the extremely reactionary regime in Russia in the 1730s during the reign of Empress Anna Ivanovna, named after her favourite, Biron, the inspiration and brains behind this regime.

dialogue as a monologue. The intellectual elites would, as usual, come up with the brilliant ideas, and the people, as always, kept silent. However, there were occasional exceptions. If the Decembrists knew little about the people and, in general, were not interested in them, then the Narodniks took a Romantic view of the masses, painting them as a kind of repository of worldly wisdom and an inflexible benchmark of moral virtue — a position which should also be treated critically.

At that time, the Russian mentality within the nation still had many features of a traditional society: the predominance of agricultural labour, an irrational type of thinking, and a collective sense of identity based on a communal lifestyle. These features of social development were reflected in the demographics of the society, in which until 1917 over 80% of the population lived in rural areas. It was precisely here, in the village, that customs and traditions were formed in accordance with a set of archetypal images. Individuation and self-identification were mainly based on the family and communal work.

The Narodniks maintained that an educated person could be misled by the numerous tangled truths produced by humankind, but the people - never - because the people draw their wisdom from the source itself.

It should be noted that village life was built upon the preservation of basic Christian morality and a clear sense of conventional wisdom. As the works of village writers and researchers such as Shukshin and Astafiev illustrate, the village had an intuitive sense of the difference between good and evil, which was rarely misguided.

With the help of the Bolsheviks, however, popular anger and discontent finally exploded. As the whirlwinds of revolution died down, permitted to have their historical word, people took advantage of a new campaign to eradicate illiteracy. The peasantry proved fertile ground, with tens of thousands of eager new scholars flocking to institutes. The country was industrialising at breakneck speed, and science was developing.

The transition to a planned economy, the transfer of industrial practice outside the institution of the family unit, the large-scale involvement of women in production and social activities and many other socio-economic changes transformed the way of life of the population. Industrialisation boosted the urban population, and a system of urban values began to take shape in which, along with traditional values, the values of education, material prosperity and career growth had a prominent role. Despite the undeniable appearance of urban values, however, these were not overtly expressed during the Soviet era, and merged quite harmoniously with traditional values (family, marriage, children and work).

Naturally, the mentality likewise changed. It became clear that the Russian mentality is based on largely ethical values; that the Russian people have a clear sense of the difference between justice and injustice and are not the least bit inclined to put these values up for sale.

However, in the early 1990s, they were asked to do just that. The *la vie en rose* of the 'capitalist paradise' seduced many, and an immediate restructuring of the value system took place. What's worse, we returned to a mindset where the people had practically no role on the historical stage.

In Russia, capitalist relations - foreign to the Russian frame of mind - were introduced, undermining ideological foundations and traditional values. As a consequence, capitalism in Russia was built based on pragmatic attitudes, whilst the moral and ethical component of social relations was largely lost. The new industrial and social relations produced a new type of person. This is the so-called 'modern consumer,' characterised by rational thinking, an urban value system where material issues take precedence over spiritual ones, hedonistic life principles, extreme individualism and pragmatism. Collective values, reflecting the essence of the traditional Russian mentality and national character in their initial form, were relegated to second or even third place.

THE RUSSIAN MENTALITY

Although the fundamental changes of the post-Soviet period transformed the value system and worldview which relates to the structural components, nevertheless, they did not affect the national mentality at its deepest level. In this regard, although the mentality of modern Russians has been transformed, its original basis remains intact, offering vital strength to overcome the mental difficulties which come in times of crisis and social instability. The Russian national character is known for such positive features as adaptability and independence, ingenuity and openness to that which is new, resilience and patience in times of adversity, warmth and consideration for friends and family. Some groups also demonstrate a passionate need for justice, to find meaning in life, to serve high ideals such as the homeland, a sense of duty, self-sacrifice and self-denial.

Thus, the mentality displays qualities of both continuity and transformation. Regardless of what angle we take, an analysis of the dynamics of mentality in Russia leads to the conclusion that the process of transformation reflects the degree of society's adaptation to changing conditions. In conditions of social stability, the mentality remains fairly stable. During such periods, the dynamics of mentality are weak, whilst the continuity of mental characteristics at an intergenerational level manifest themselves most strongly. Mentality is subject to active transformation during periods of crisis in the social system associated with its overhaul or reorganisation.

V.V. KOZLOV

THE MENTALITIES OF VARIOUS COUNTRIES AND PEOPLES

The differences in the mentalities of various countries and peoples.

Over the course of many decades, whilst preserving its own distinctive identity, Russia has become more and more similar to Western countries. A modern, large Russian city is often visually indistinguishable from a foreign metropolis, with the same fast-food chains, huge shopping centres, and people in droves taking out loans and using social media. Until fairly recently, this would have been hard to believe, but now it's a fact of everyday life. Despite many similarities, however, there are distinct cultural differences between Russia and Western countries. But what lies behind them? What prevents Russians from becoming more like Americans or Europeans? (And is this something worth doing?) The answer to these questions is as simple as it is complex. Specifically, it is a matter of mentality.

From the characteristics outlined by a number of researchers, it follows that strict and repressive governance has played a huge role in shaping the Russian mentality. Nevertheless, bearing in mind the existence of a typology of mentality in accordance with Western and Eastern cultures, it should be noted that the Russian mentality has shifted towards the West. This conclusion may be supported by turning to the various criteria customarily used to analyse a particular mentality, thereby identifying it as either Western or Eastern.

The Soviet era, which gave birth to a new individual, was suddenly replaced by another, which marked a renewal of the economic, political and socio-cultural milieu. The collapse of the Soviet government and the state went hand-in-hand with a radical restructuring of the economy. The introduction of capitalist relations necessitated a change in the value system of post-Soviet society, and the formation of a new worldview in keeping with this stage of development. The pro-Western model of organising the social system became, for certain segments of the population, a reference point in relation to both the cultural subsystem (values, worldview) and family and marriage practices. In essence, an attempt was made to introduce elements of a Western-style mentality into Russian society.

It's worth pointing out that many Russians had absolutely no desire to change or embrace anything, be it capitalism or private enterprise. Of course, we too have our share of 'bad asses' and 'tough guys,' but they are not a class of the bourgeoisie who are dynamic and feel a sense of responsibility towards the country. The bourgeoisie existed for a short time before the Revolution, but so far it is virtually non-existent in Russia. This is one of the problems: the process of forming a middle class in Russia which must not only become the foundation of civil society but also the backbone of the state, is not only incomplete, it has just started, and the country must go through this stage.

The roots of this problem lie in the past. Many Russian thinkers, philosophers and writers have noted that Russians have an inherent antipathy to anything bourgeois. All of them vehemently rejected bourgeois vulgarity and self-satisfied ignorance. The hatred of their free spirit for the bourgeoisie as a class, for the 'bourgeois plebeian' as an anthropological type in the words of Berdyaev, was the life spring from which their reflections and prophecies about Russia drew inspiration.

Russians never regarded the institution of private property as something sacred. Property is not an absolute good; on the contrary, it is often an evil, a sin, a break with the Evangelical Christ who condemned it. In the Old Believer prayer of the Russians, Ephraim the Syrian says: 'Lord, wring from me the sins of despondency and avarice.' Therefore, 'the soul of Russia is not a bourgeois soul. The soul of the Russian people,' Berdyaev wrote, 'has never worshipped the golden calf — and I believe it will never worship it... A Russian will rob and cheat and profit in dishonest ways, but he will never regard material wealth as the highest value... A Russian bourgeois, while making money and enriching himself, always feels a bit sinful, and can't help but despise bourgeois virtues.'[18] Berdyaev believed that a Russian defines his attitude to 'property and theft' through his 'attitude to people.' From this he extrapolated the Russian antipathy to the bourgeoisie and the rejection of bourgeois values.

For example, in the view of many Russians, business is theft. Beyond the Ring Road, outside Moscow people have very different values, and they want the state to leave them alone. This means they are not citizens, but a populace; and millions of Russians are a populace. What kind of civil society and civil initiatives are we talking about?

By way of comparison, the structure of the public consciousness of people from other cultures clearly differs from ours, and the same is true of the domestic sphere. It would be hard to imagine, for example, that in the midst of a heated domestic dispute in a Russian kitchen, a woman would break a cup, and her husband would respond with something like, 'why did you damage my property?' To an American, however, such a response would seem completely normal.

The American believes that everyone should do their own thing. There's not much chance you can get him to crawl under a broken-down car because, after all, that's what the car repair shop is for. Likewise, he won't bake a pizza or make a pie — for that there are bakeries and pizzerias. More and more Americans are even eating breakfast outside of the home. Almost everyone has a coffee machine at home, but on the way to work they will stop at a coffee shop. If an American does something with his own hands, it is only that which he knows how to do professionally.

---

18   Berdyaev N. The Fate of Russia. Moscow: EKSMO-PRESS, Kharkiv: Folio. 1999.

THE RUSSIAN MENTALITY

Otherwise, he prefers to earn money and pay a specialist to do this work. The American economy is built on this mindset, and if many people started solving household problems with their own hands (like the Russians), their economy would collapse.

An American man won't get married just because he's passionately in love; he will get married when he has created a base for a family. In the meantime, the happy couple will just live in a basement and get used to a future life together in marriage. Each one will pay their own way in a restaurant, pay their share of the rent, the utilities and the grocery costs. Many continue this practice even after wedlock. An American woman has many more rights in the home than does her husband. If a husband forces his wife to engage in sexual relations with him against her will, he can be charged with rape.

If, in casual conversation, an American should ask how you're doing, Heaven forbid you should reply, 'like shit,' and then elaborate on the details. Your shit is your problem, and there's no way they will let themselves get bogged down in your mess. On the other hand, they won't burden you with their problems either; they will solve them by themselves.

In Russia, things work a little differently. For us, a friend is much more than just someone we communicate with on a daily basis; a friend is a personal psychologist, adviser and soulmate rolled into one. They share your defeats and your victories. They are always there to lend an ear. Sometimes, just talking about something is enough to let off some steam, reduce the tension, and give you the strength to keep going. In the States, even close friends keep their distance. It's considered poor taste to pour out one's soul to a friend and share intimate problems. After all, there are paid specialists, psychologists for this.

Let's take a look at some fundamental principles of the Western mentality, one of which is encapsulated in the word, 'enjoy.'

The goal of Westerners is to enjoy life at all costs. It is precisely to enjoy life more that they work, because by earning more money you can purchase the best things in life (the best food, housing, travel, etc.).

Another principle of the Western mentality is not to interfere with the enjoyment of others. This is why Westerners always appear very attentive and friendly to one another, and try to ensure that their own enjoyment does not interfere with that of others. As long as it remains within the confines of the law, do as you wish, no one will say a word. It's your right.

The third cornerstone of the Western mentality involves complying with laws and regulations. Immigrants living in Western European countries always take note of this point. Everything is done according to the proper order, and rules are to be followed to the letter. Even at two o'clock in the morning on an empty street, many people stand at a red traffic light waiting for it to turn green, although there are no cars in sight and no other pedestrians. They are used to getting on a bus only through the front doors and using the back doors to exit, as well as pressing the button to signal a stop. As for the buses themselves, they are supposed to keep to a strict schedule.

Following the rules ensures peace and order. If prostitution is legal in the country (as in Germany, for instance), then no one will say a word if you choose to make a career out of it. A German will never leave things to chance, an American will seek justice in the courts which protect human rights and are guaranteed by the Constitution on the basis of a 'sacred' contract between citizens and the authorities they have elected. As for the victory of good over evil, in Western culture this is in the hands of political parties and depends on their ideas about what is good and what is evil; and, most importantly, it depends on the personal efforts of each member of society.

Some people maintain that the Russian mentality is based on a physiological feature: supposedly, Slavs have a more developed right hemisphere of the brain, which is responsible for emotions, and not for logic;

THE RUSSIAN MENTALITY

therefore, we are often irrational. Scientists have thus far had nothing to say either way on the anatomical specificity of the Slavs, but this feature of the Russian mentality is clearly visible in matters of planning — say, the family budget, for instance. If a German meticulously calculates all expenses up to and including the purchase of tissues for a month, six months, or even a year, then to a Russian, such an approach would be completely alien.

Any consideration of the Russian mentality can't help but note such features as sentimentality and compassion. Whereas people of other nationalities know how to keep their distance, we immediately empathise with others; hence such Russian expressions as 'heart-to-heart conversation' and 'heartfelt exchange.'

An Italian will never discuss family problems with a stranger, and an American will avoid personal topics. Russians, on the other hand, have few reservations about pouring their hearts out in conversation. Often, on the very first day of an acquaintance, we are ready to share our innermost feelings with someone, and we are very perceptive of other's joys and misfortunes.

During a trip to Italy with my family in a rented car, the following happened: The car got a flat tyre, and the jack turned out to be broken. For an hour, we attempted to flag down a car on the road, but to no avail. Italians sped by without pulling over — it was not their problem. Then, an hour later, a miracle of miracles occurred: a car pulled over. Behind the wheel was an Italian, and next to him was his Russian wife. They helped us change the tyre and took us to the nearest garage, where we had it repaired. They spent another hour helping perfect strangers, and managing this whole process was a compassionate Russian woman.

That's why practically every Russian immigrant who has gone to Western Europe, the United States or Canada can't get used to the fact that people around them are cold, reserved and distant. It takes years to establish close relationships. In Russia, people are much warmer and more open, and relationships develop much faster.

There's a downside to our sensitivity, though, for whilst we are quickly drawn to people, we often become disillusioned with them just as fast. These features of the Russian mentality help explain why our relationships are subject to such abrupt changes — fraternising after a fight, for example, and vice versa. And yet, if a fight or a serious grievance does occur, a Russian will soon put it behind them. There is no tradition of 'blood feuds' or 'blood revenge' in Russia, since holding a grudge isn't a feature of the mentality. As Dostoevsky put it: 'The entire Russian people are ready to forget their torments for one kind word.'[19]

In Western society, people prefer to keep their distance — to keep their moods, both good and bad, to themselves, and to conceal everything behind a polite smile. I respect your personal space, you respect mine, and in this way we will manage to co-exist. Distance helps mitigate the hostility between people. By contrast, we Russians are not used to keeping our distance from one another — we either openly love or hate without measure. When we are happy, we want to share our joy with others; when we feel bad, we won't put on a façade for the sake of politeness — we make it clear: danger, do not approach!

As for negative Russian qualities, the philosopher, Lossky wrote about them as follows: 'The negative characteristics of the Russian people are extremism, maximalism, the demand that it be all or nothing, lack of firm character, no discipline, audacious testing of values, anarchism... nihilism.' Faith in the future 'cancels out the present, the work to preserve it leads to a negation of what has already been achieved, to jumping from one extreme to another.'[20]

In our country, therefore, 'all moderate forms of culture (for example, the ideal of an enlightened monarchy, the Constitution, the rule of

---

19   F. Dostoevsky. Notes from the Underground. — M.: AST, 2016.
20   Lossky N. O. The Conditions of Absolute Good, — Moscow, 1991.

law, liberalism, ideological and cultural pluralism, political tolerance and compromise, bourgeois market relations, etc.) were eradicated, forced out of society without receiving support at either the "lower" or "top" levels, among the conservatives, or amongst the ranks of the revolutionaries.'[21]

The attitude of Russians to government power is fundamentally different from that in the West. A Western citizen respects power, but that power exists not by and for itself; it is there to serve them, otherwise such power comes to an abrupt end. A Russian citizen, on the other hand, has an inclination toward totalitarianism, nepotism and fawning over the current government. This is not a matter limited to political views; once a Russian gains at least some kind of power, they almost always to some extent become a tyrant, be it a state ruler, a manager at a production facility, or simply a janitor or a moderator on a forum.

Another feature of the Russian mentality is social conformity. We are very concerned about how others see us, always trying to ensure others don't think badly of us. For instance, when leaving a hostel only a Russian woman would think of cleaning the room before the maid arrives. A French or German woman knows perfectly well this is the job of the cleaner — it's what they're paid to do!

Despite our creative thinking, our way of doing things can be described as conservative. We are wary of innovations, and it takes a great deal of time to gradually allow them into our lives. Research shows that 55% of elderly people in the UK know how to use a computer, 67% in the USA, but only 24% in Russia. This is not simply because they can't afford to purchase the equipment, but also because they are reluctant to change their usual way of life. Russians are often conservative and do not wish to try new ways of spending their free time.

Western sociological studies have suggested the Russian mentality is similar to that of Northern Europeans. However, in the last 20 years most

---

21   Lossky N. O. The Conditions of Absolute Good, — Moscow, 1991.

Russians have taken a step back and become more traditional. Likewise, there are still significant cultural differences between Russians and Europeans.

There is statistical data gathered using psychological tests in cross-cultural studies to support this. K. Kasyanova applied the MMPI[22] test to Russian students and a control group of pilots, comparing her data with the results obtained by other psychologists from many countries. Her study found that Russians are overwhelmingly 'cycloidal' in terms of personality. This is a concept from psychoanalysis, meaning that Russians are disinclined to systematically perform activities which do not depend on mood, unlike, for instance, the punctual Germans.[23]

Some fascinating cross-cultural research findings were obtained by E. Danilova, E. Dubitskaya and M. Tararukhina. They used a psychological test developed by the Dutch social psychologist, Geert Hofstede in the 1960s to measure organisational cultural parameters.[24]

Hofstede identified the ethnic and national features of labour relations and refuted the belief in their universality. Using the Hofstede test, 70 nations have been studied. In recent years, mass testing of Russians has been conducted: 1,700 respondents were employees of power companies in 23 regions of Russia, and 518 employees of large machine-production facilities in Moscow, the Volga region, and the Vladimir region. The engineers included many progressive, forward-thinking managers and specialists, whilst 90% of the machine builders were ordinary Russian workers.

---

22 The Minnesota Multiphasic Personality Inventory(MMPI) is a questionnaire created in the early 1940s by Starke Hathaway and John McKinley at the University of Minnesota, and designed to study individual characteristics and mental states of the individual. MMPI is the most studied and one of the most popular psycho-diagnostic methods, and is widely used in clinical practice.
23 Yadov V. A. Regarding the National Specificity of the Modernisation of Russian Society. IS RAS, 2009.
24 V. A. Yadov, Clement K. et al. The Impact of Western Sociocultural Models on Social Practices in Russia. IS RAS, 2009.

THE RUSSIAN MENTALITY

What were the results of these studies? It transpired that the Danes, Norwegians and Finns form a single block, which Dubitskaya and Tararukhina called the 'Northern European solidarity syndrome.' The English, Americans, Irish, Germans, Austrians, Italians and Swiss formed another statistical cluster, which was referred to as the 'Romano-Germanic achievement syndrome.' Russia was grouped with the Northern Europeans. (These results indicate which kind of political and economic form could take root in Russia — an Anglo-Saxon type of liberalism, a Southern European paternalism, or a Scandinavian socialism).

The researchers defined another scale using management terminology as 'loyalty to the company in exchange for guarantees.' In a broad sense, this represents a mentality of dependence on the external environment, or, on the contrary, a mentality that draws on the social subject's own resources. According to management logic, the first is the mentality of an employee, and the second is that of a partner. Based on this index, Russians are among those who most value guarantees from an organisation. On the whole, they conclude that the Russian cultural matrix (recall the matrix of labour relations) is far from that of the Romano-Germans and again is most similar to the mentality of employees in Northern Europe.

Russian organisational culture is built on two pillars: solidarity between employees and subordination to the organisation. On the Hofstede test scale, this is referred to as a culture of 'femininity': caring for one another, intuition, and valuing free time. At the opposite pole is 'masculinity': drive and determination, rationalism, perseverance in achieving goals, and money as a driving force.

'Subordination to the organisation in the culture of labour relations is associated with a well-known feature of the Russian mentality — etatism, an attitude to the state as its subject, not as a free citizen. In practice, this means loyalty to the existing order in exchange for guarantees from the state, sociologists conclude.[25]

---

25   URL: https://www.psychologos.ru

In comparison to Asian, African, and Latin American countries, the value system in Russia is quite close to that of Western Europe, 'but it is more conservative, traditional, has a tendency to be more hierarchal, and is less inclined to individual rights and freedoms.'[26] On the whole, Western and Russian sociologists didn't discover anything new here. A more interesting question is: has there been a transformation of values in Russia over the past 20 years? This topic has also been studied.

In the 1990s, an evident shift in values occurred towards a 'modern personality' (intellectual autonomy, the value of skill), especially among the younger generations. However, in the period from 2000 to 2005, there was an increase in hedonism as opposed to the values of developing creative ability. On most important fronts, the country took a step back, and the cultural prerequisites for modernisation deteriorated. According to monitoring research conducted in 1998, 2004 and 2007 by the Sociology Institute of the Russian Academy of Sciences, in the period from 2004 to 2007, the share of so-called modernists declined from 26% to 20%, and that of traditionalists increased from 41% to 47%, whilst the share of 'intermediates' remained steady at 33%.

Signs of 'modernity,' in the view of the authors, involved accepting the values of individual freedom, which is 'completely unacceptable' to traditionalists and intermediates (80% of those questioned). 'In their view,' writes M. K. Gorshkov,[27] 'the optimal model of Russian development is etacratic, which is based on the omnipotence of the state, and ideally serves to express the interests of society as a whole, ensuring the security of each individual citizen and the community.'

Other studies reveal the progressively declining value of patience as a component of charity and humanism in post-Soviet Russia. Thus, re-

---

26   Russian Society and the Challenges of the Time / ed. by M. Gorshkov and V. Petukhova. — M : Ves Mir, 2017.

27   Mikhail Konstantinovich Gorshkov is a Soviet and Russian sociologist, Doctor of philosophy, academician of the Russian Academy of Sciences, Director of the Sociology Institute of the Russian Academy of Sciences, Editor-in-chief of the scientific network journal, "Bulletin of the Institute of Sociology," and the journal, "Sociological Science and Social Practice".

THE RUSSIAN MENTALITY

search by N. I. Lapina[28] demonstrates the changes in the structure of basic Russian values during the period from 1990 to 2006. In 1990, the traditional value of self-sacrifice ranked eighth among the fourteen basic values, by 1994 it had dropped to eleventh, and by 2006 it had fallen further still, increasingly giving way to such modern values as independence and initiative.

Opinion surveys show that the 'cultural component' of the Russian mentality is still far from that of Europe. Cultural attitudes to 'exceptions from the norm' in modern Russia are examined in the works of S. S. Yaroshenko (attitudes to the poor) and I. N. Tartakovskaya (gender stereotypes and lifestyles). A study by T. A. Dobrovolskaya and N. B. Shabalina noted the intolerance of Russian respondents to the very idea of co-existence with people outside the norm. The respondents expressed their distaste for the idea of having a disabled person as a relative (39%), a neighbour (37%), a boss (29%), a government representative (27%), a subordinate (22%), or their child's teacher (20%).

What conclusions can be drawn from these studies? In general, under favourable circumstances (a democratic government, respect for individual rights, integration into the Western world), Russians are potentially ready to become 'Northern Europeans' (in the same sense as the Finns, who a mere hundred years ago were akin to Russians and who transformed into Europeans in a very short space of time by the standards of world history). For now, however, all of this is pie in the sky. Such are the realities of life in today's Russia, whereas a survival tactic in a hostile environment, for the average Russian the only saviour is the state.

There is yet another nuance, however. Dmitry Trenin, head of the Moscow Carnegie Centre believes that the 'Russian political elite does not see itself under someone. The Swiss elite or even the German elite feels great where it is, but not the Russian elite. At one time, the German

---

[28] N. I. Lapin. Sociocultural Factors of Russian Stagnation and Modernisation // New Ideas in Sociology / Resp. ed. J. T. Toshchenko. — M.: UNITY-DANA, 2013.

elite had its backbone broken, and was then completely restructured. This was not the case with the Russian elite after 1991, despite the defeat of the Soviet Union in the Cold War. Perhaps the Russian elite would fare better if it ceded some of its sovereignty (following the example of the EU countries), or maybe not, but the fact remains, and there's no escaping it.'[29]

A very interesting question is how Russian citizens are treated abroad. In most countries, Russian tourists are treated either neutrally, like any other guests, or well, that is, shown particular warmth and attention.

Resorts in various parts of the world owe their existence to the fact that at a certain time they became fashionable among Russian tourists who began travelling en masse to this or that particular place. In recent years, Russian tourists have played a significant role in the development of the tourism industry in many countries.

It is commonly thought that Russians are heavy drinkers, much more so than any other nation. However, statistics regarding alcohol abuse among young people in Europe presented at a meeting of Health Ministers of the European Union held in Luxembourg in 2016 prove this is false. In general, the statistics point to the fact that young people are drinking more and more, and starting to do so at an earlier age. The ministers underscored that excessive consumption of beer, which has become a huge problem in EU countries of late, poses a particular health hazard. In Denmark, 43% of teenagers aged 15 drink beer every day, in Greece 42%, and in the UK 40% (but in Wales 50%). It's noteworthy that in nearly all EU countries, 15-year-old girls drink stronger alcohol than boys. Typically, the majority of alcohol consuming boys and girls have already drunk themselves 'to the point of unconsciousness' on numerous occasions. In all European countries, more than a thousand young people aged 15 to 29 die annually as a result of alcohol abuse.

---

29   March 15, 2018, Source: Medusa

THE RUSSIAN MENTALITY

World ranking by alcohol consumption[30]

Place	Country	Consumption
1	Moldova	15.2
2	Lithuania	15.0
3	Czech Republic	14.4
4	Germany	13.4
5	Nigeria	13.4
6	Ireland	13.0
7	Luxembourg	13.0
8	Latvia	12.9
9–12	Bulgaria, Romania, France, Slovenia	12.7–12.6
13, 14, 15	Portugal, Belgium, Gabon	12.3–11.
16	Russia	11.7

In light of this, EU Health Ministers have once again appealed to the producers of alcoholic beverages, asking that they voluntarily commit to not producing advertising campaigns targeting young people.

When asked by a reporter, 'What is the difference between a Russian and a Westerner?' one modern researcher of the Russian national character, the famous writer, Vladimir Lichutin (born in 1940), replied as follows: 'The Russian is a child of vast, open spaces, a person of freedom and will. The Westerner has got freedom, but he has forgotten what it means to live unbounded; for the European it is enough that his gaze reaches the church and his house — in this, he sees stability and security. The European is gutless; he was only too willing to lie down under Hitler, offering almost no resistance. The sacrificial Russian liberated Europe from oppression, and now, smug and well-fed, it arrogantly laughs at us. For Russians, the will is higher and more desirable than freedom; and now, under the pressure of foreigners and outsiders, we are losing our will, and we yearn for it. In the search for freedom, thousands of Russian men rushed to Siberia to create a life without force and violence...

---

30 World Health Organisation: Global Status Report on Alcohol and Health 2018.

This desire in Russians for unlimited will gave birth to such national qualities as patience, the ability to make do with only that which is most necessary, non-possessiveness, contemplation, and a sense of collective unity... From the desire for will stems the eternal conflict of the state and the people... For Russians, to give up their will is equivalent to cutting off the soul, transforming it into a kind of *peau de chagrin*. It is from the desire for will that the conflict between the "democrats" and the Russians arose, for the democrats (pro-Westerners) have no such desire. For them, the "kitchen counter" version of freedom is more than enough, so long as no one raises a hand against their homes and other personal property... From this stems the difference in aspirations and the different perception of homeland.'[31]

The differences in the mentalities of various countries and peoples (continued, values)

The famous Russian philosopher, Ivan Ilyin wrote: 'We know that Western peoples do not understand and cannot tolerate Russian identity. They view a single Russian state as an obstacle to their commercial, linguistic and territorial expansion. They intend to divide the all-Russian "broom" into twigs, break these twigs one by one, and use them to kindle the dying flame of their civilisation. They need to dismember Russia in order to lead it through the Western equalisation and undoing, and thus destroy it: a plan of hatred and lust for power...

'Russia is not human dust and not chaos. It is, first and foremost, a great nation which has not squandered its strength or lost faith in its calling. These people are starved of a free order, for peaceful labour, for property and for national culture. Do not, therefore, bury them prematurely!'[32]

---

31   Lichutin V. V. Reflections on the Russian People. — M.: Institute of Russian Civilisation, 2013.
32   URL: https://oko-planet.su

THE RUSSIAN MENTALITY

A mysterious duality can be found in everything in Russia. Countless numbers of theses and antitheses can be established about the Russian national character, and many contradictions identified in the Russian soul. On the one hand, for instance, there is humility, compassion and a thirst for freedom, and on the other rebellion, cruelty and an inclination towards slavery. As I. Bunin wrote, 'We, Russians are like wood: you can fashion both a club and an icon from us.' Belinsky makes a similar point: 'If it works, pray to it; if it doesn't, it's good for covering pots.'

In his story, "Small Fry," published in 1907, A. I. Kuprin stated: 'It's as though this expectation of a miracle were in the blood of the entire Russian people.... You may approach a man with mathematics, a car, political economy, medicine... he will not believe anything that is simple and clear. He killed doctors during smallpox and cholera epidemics, organised potato riots, and beat surveyors with stakes.... But whisper to him, just whisper one word in his ear: "the golden letter," or "Antichrist," or "he has arrived," and he immediately pulls the banner from his spade, and is willing to go to certain death. You may draw him into any, the most stupid, the most ridiculous, the most disgusting, the bloodiest sect, and he will follow you. It's unbelievable!'

Describing extreme manifestations of the "dark" side of the Russian mentality, in his story "A Dozen Knives in the Back of the Revolution," A. Averchenko noted: 'Rash is the Russian fool — Oh, how rash... What good is it that later, when his joyous excitement passes, he will stupidly cry leaden tears long and hard over the broken church and over the shattered finances and over the already dead science; at least now everyone is looking at the fool! At least now he is the centre of merry attention, this same fool that no one took any notice of before.'

Ilyin also pointed out this duality and these contradictions in Russian life and the minds of the Russian people: 'The whole history of Russia is a struggle between two gravitational forces: one which is centripetal and creative, and one which is centrifugal and decomposing; between a sacrificial, disciplining statehood and an individualising, anarchic instinct.'[33]

In essence, the reasoning of Russian liberals about the acceptable path of development for Russia goes something like this: We strive to be like the West not because the West is good, but because the alternative is worse. Either we become part of the global process, or the road along which this process takes place.

Yes, we live in a global world, and we are deeply engaged in cooperation with Western countries, but we must not forget that we live in Russia. Whilst broadly cooperating with the world around us, we must never lose sight of the fact that we are Russian.

It is commonly thought that Russia is neither the West nor the East, but always a bridge between them. In the course of conducting a comparative analysis of Russian and Western civilisations, we must answer the question: does Russian civilisation exist? This is all the more important because for a quarter of a century Russian students have been studying Russian history from textbooks (edited by L. I. Semennikova) according to which there is no distinctive Russian civilisation. Is it a 'bridge' between the civilisations of the East and the West, a transitional space, or something else altogether?

Criticising the 'bridge' concept, some political scientists argue that you cannot live on a bridge, you must live on the shore, choose a side — this one or that one.

Russian Orthodox archpriest and doctor of philosophy, Dimitri Leskin believes that we are not Asia, but we are definitely not Europe. We are different, and Russia has always been different. The Russian path is not along the main road; it is marginal. The specificity of Russian civilisation is such that it will be impossible to adapt it to European ideals. Russia was formed as a country of global interests.

---

[33] Artemova V. G., Filippova Ya. V. The Mentality of the Russian People: Traditions and Evolution. Nizhny Novgorod state University named after N. I. Lobachevsky. 2008.

It is possible to reprogram a person through education, but there is no way to ever undo the genetic code. Despite all its European modernisation, China will never become European; China will always remain China.

Some people believe that the resettlement of groups of people around the world (united based on tribal and labour principles) was due to a desire to avoid influence from other groups and to remain themselves. Therefore, possibly, humankind will not want to dissolve into an all-embracing humanity; perhaps, it may not even be able to do so. Many Russians who moved to the West during the first, second and third waves of immigration were never able to completely forget their Russian identity.

As is well-known, Fyodor Dostoevsky was a staunch critic of Europe and Western Christianity, glorifying Russian Messianism and pan-Slavism. His friend, the Russian philosopher Vladimir Solovyov, whilst defending the Western Church in every possible way, highlighted two dangers for the 'Russian world': cosmopolitanism and nationalism — when the people become the enemy of humanity.

Friedrich Nietzsche, a fierce critic of Western civilisation, looked to Russia with hope. Oswald Spengler, meanwhile, spoke of the 'decline of Europe,' but he did not mean Russia.

The German philosopher, Martin Heidegger[34] called Russia 'the land of the future… the only country that can save Europe… It is from the depths of its unparalleled sufferings that it will draw an equally profound knowledge of people and the meaning of life in order to proclaim it to the peoples of the Earth. Russians have to this end the spiritual prerequisites that no other European peoples today have.'[35]

In his book, *Europe and the Soul of the East*, the German professor, Walter Schubart wrote: 'The West gave humanity the most advanced

---

34   Martin Heidegger (1889–1976) was a German idealist philosopher who gave a new direction to German and global philosophy, and is one of the greatest philosophers of the XX century.
35   URL: https://subscribe.ru

types of technology, statehood and communication, but took away its soul. The task of Russia is to return the soul to mankind. It is Russia that has the powers that Europe has lost or destroyed in itself... The Western European regards life as though it were a slave on whose neck he has placed his foot... He does not look with devotion at the sky, but full of lust for power, looks down upon the Earth with an evil and hostile gaze. The Russian is driven not by a will to power, but by a sense of reconciliation and love. He is filled not with anger and hatred, but with a most profound trust in the essence of the world. He sees in mankind not an enemy, but a brother... The Englishman wants to see the world as a factory, the Frenchman as a salon, the German as a barracks, the Russian as a temple... The Englishman seeks booty, the Frenchman fame, the German power, the Russian, sacrifice. The Englishman wants to cash in on those close to him, the Frenchman to make an impression on them, the German to command them, whereas the Russian doesn't want anything from them. He does not want to transform his neighbour into a means to an end. This is the brotherhood of the Russian heart and the Russian idea, and this is the Gospel of the future. The Russian universal man is the bearer of a new solidarity. Promethean man is already doomed to death. The age of Saint John is dawning — an age of the man of love and freedom. This is the future of the Russian people. The West is driven by a lack of belief, fear and self-love, whereas the Russian soul is driven by faith, peace, and a sense of brotherhood. This is precisely why the future belongs to Russia.'[36]

---

36 Walter Schubart, (1897–1942) — German philosopher. Schubart W. Europe and the Soul of the East / The Social Sciences and Modernity. M., 1992, No. 6; 1993, No. 1–4; prev. G. Böll — 1995 No. 4, 1995.

GENETIC, CULTURAL CODE, ARCHETYPES[37]

It is highly unlikely that the West and the East will ever reach a consensus in their dispute about fundamental values; nonetheless, it is important to understand the reasons behind the differences.

The Western archetype is based on fundamental materialism, which identifies the individual with the material world at the level of the unconscious. This identification produces a corresponding type of consciousness — a rational worldview as an ideal reflection of the system of physical laws of the revealed world. In particular, the rational worldview means submission to all its laws. Projected onto public relations, this produces the so-called 'civil society,' which is based on a law-respecting, law-abiding type of citizen. Finally, by identifying the individual with the material, fundamental materialism makes the sense of personal material property seem organic.

All this makes the Westerner disinclined either to steal or to give away that which is theirs, since at a subconscious level, they view property as something sacred. This is a person perfectly adapted to transform the material world, as this is their form of self-realisation: they are by nature a worker. They are a people for whom it is natural to follow the laws of the country they live in since this comes from the subconscious. They don't tend to ask themselves questions such as 'why?' and 'what for?', since rational consciousness is always finite and bound by what is already known. This is precisely why they are unable to go beyond these boundaries: the romance of travelling into the unknown is not their cup of tea. This is neither good nor bad; it's just the way it is.

---

37   The term 'archetype' (from the Greek, arche — beginning, typos) was introduced into psychology by Carl Jung, who defines the archetype as the original, innate mental structures which form the content of the collective unconscious and which are the basis of the universal symbolism of fantasies.

What has been said should not be taken too literally. The terms 'Eastern' and 'Western' do not refer to geography alone: people with such mentalities may reside anywhere, although we traditionally associate the corresponding types of societies with the Eastern or Western worlds, respectively. We are speaking about the manifestations of an archetype not as a pure embodiment of it in specific personalities, which are almost always a mixture of various things, but as dominants in behaviour.

Unlike the Western archetype, the Eastern archetype is irrational, since it is based on the identification of the individual with the ideal which always lies beyond the boundaries of the known, and therefore does not follow the laws of the rational world. By nature, the Easterner is not law-abiding — this is inherent in their irrationality. They will never, for instance, build a civil society in their country, and will always lead it between autocracy and anarchy. It is precisely this quality, however, which enables them able to overcome laws and create the impossible from the point of view of the Western world, both good and evil.

Material goods beyond the basic necessities cannot, by definition, be the main motivating factor for them. In search of such motivating factors, they always ask 'why?' and 'what for?', and look for irrational answers. Conventional wisdom, such as 'it's necessary,' 'it's the law' or 'everyone does it' just don't cut it. If they are unable to strike a balance between the subject in question and the subconscious 'I,' they will not accept this subject as their own, and without accepting it they will not dedicate themselves to it fully. They will not work like a dog for the sake of personal material well-being, preferring instead to live in disorder rather than exhausting themselves amassing 'Earthly treasures.' They are able to penetrate the unknown, expanding the boundaries of their knowledge of the world around them. This is what gives the Easterner the upper hand over the "blinkered" Westerner.

THE RUSSIAN MENTALITY

It is possible to draw an analogy between the division of East and West and the contrast between an infant and an adult. We all live in the same material world with its rational laws; one who has learnt and accepted these laws is like an adult, wise with the experience of life. They are the absolute master of this world, effective and successful, but they are also arrogant, strict and moralising towards silly children who live, to their minds, in some fictional and incomprehensible world. Indeed, children are not of this world, but, living in it and trying to adapt to it they put a great deal of faith in what adults do and say.

Russia's problem is that, yet again, it is having purely Western and therefore alien ideas forced upon it: the ideas of material wealth and of personal freedom, which are always based on pride — the root of all sin in the Christian worldview. Neither of these ideas will ever take root in the Eastern mentality of most Russians. Therefore, instead of honest and selfless work to help bring them about, they will always give rise to fraud and theft, and instead of a civil sense of justice, arbitrariness and anarchy. Those in power can endlessly change the forms of government, write and rewrite laws or reshuffle officials, but until society finds its generic idea, it will live in timelessness.

Main conclusions on the materials presented in chapters 5 to 7

Modern social psychology suggests that mentality is not immutable, noting a correlation between changes in living conditions and social relations and changes in mentality.

Undoubtedly, people have their own national and ethnic specifics. However, it's hard to ignore the defining role played by our social relations and the social environment in which we live. Changes in the social environment produce changes in mentality.

In the last 100 years, Russia has changed three times, and has done so qualitatively. Accordingly, people shaped by 'fundamentally different conditions' must be fundamentally different.

Of course, the mentality of any nation finds its expression through models of perception and behaviour, which affect the political and economic life of the country. Moreover, this mentality is based on historical experience. For instance, peoples may perceive the same event from entirely different perspectives because of their different mentalities. Each people will have their own truth, and to attempt to change this will be a largely thankless task.

Mentality is transformed as individuals in a society and society as a whole undergo changes in consciousness. The mentality of the Russian people has undergone a long evolutionary path, having experienced many significant changes while retaining its mental core. This is because mentality is formed under the influence of climatic, religious, and geographical factors, which are its essential foundation. The second group of factors are socio-situational. They presuppose a situational behavioural rationality through awareness of reality, resulting in the formation of values and stereotypes. The socio-situational level of mentality overlays the fundamental basis and it is this level that is more subject to change.

In Russia, capitalist relations - foreign to the Russian frame of mind - were introduced, undermining ideological foundations and traditional values. As a consequence, capitalism in Russia was built based on pragmatic attitudes, whilst the moral and ethical component of social relations was to some extent lost. The new industrial and social relations produced a new type of person. This is the so-called 'modern consumer,' characterised by rational thinking, an urban value system where material values take precedence over spiritual ones, hedonistic life principles, extreme individualism, and pragmatism. In this character, collective values, reflecting the essence of the traditional Russian mentality and national character in their initial form, are relegated in importance.

THE RUSSIAN MENTALITY

Although the fundamental changes in the post-Soviet period transformed the value system and worldview, which relates to the structural components, nevertheless, they did not affect it at the core level. Although the mentality of modern Russians has been greatly transformed, its original basis remains intact, offering a source of strength. Thus, the mentality displays qualities of both continuity and transformation. The process of transformation reflects the degree of society's adaptation to changing conditions. In times of social stability, the mentality remains fairly stable. During such periods, the dynamics of mentality in society are weak, whilst the continuity of mental characteristics at the intergenerational level is strongly pronounced. Mentality is subject to active transformation during periods of crisis in the social system.

The Soviet era, which gave birth to a new individual, was suddenly replaced by another era, which marked a renewal of the economy, politics and the socio-cultural milieu. The collapse of the Soviet government and the state regime went hand-in-hand with a radical restructuring of the economic system. The introduction of capitalist relations necessitated a change in the value system of post-Soviet society, as well as the formation of a new worldview in keeping with this stage of development. The pro-Western model of organising the social system turned out to be an unnatural reference point in relation to both the cultural subsystem (values, worldview) and family and marriage practices. It was a doomed attempt to introduce elements of a Western-style mentality into Russian society.

In Western society, people prefer to keep their distance and to conceal everything beneath a veneer. Russians are not used to keeping their distance from one another — they either openly love or hate without measure. They prefer to share their joy or unhappiness.

A well-known feature of the Russian mentality is etatism - an attitude to the state as its subject, not as a free citizen. In practice, this means loyalty to the existing order in exchange for guarantees from the state.

The problem of modern Russia is that it is once again having purely Western ideas, which are alien to the majority of the population, forced upon it: the ideas of material wealth and personal freedom, which are always based on pride — the root of all sins according to the Christian worldview. The Eastern mentality of most Russians finds both these ideas hard to accept.

Today, Russia finds itself under an attack aimed at introducing 'Western values' into the country, and we must understand we are being asked to change archetypes. Once again, we have come to the Rubicon and find ourselves at a crossroads. Whilst we are still on this side of it by virtue of our 'Eastern irrationality,' we cannot help but ask ourselves: 'why do we need this?' The answer to this question can only be found on a personal level within oneself.

LAW AND JUSTICE

In A. P. Chekhov's story, "A Malefactor," a barefoot and thin peasant, Denis Grigoriev, is put on trial. He is accused of unscrewing a nut that attaches the rails to the tracks. The peasant does not deny doing this, but sees no fault in it. The investigator learns that Denis, just like the other men, unscrews nuts in order to make them sinkers for fishing gear. He accuses Denis of sabotage, but the defendant is genuinely unable to understand how his acts can lead to a train accident and deaths, since they 'unscrew wisely, leaving every second nut… Likewise, we must judge wisely and fairly,' he tells the investigator. The investigator sends the malefactor to prison, but Denis still does not understand what he did wrong — it's not like he put a log across the railway track.

In another story by Chekhov, "The Chameleon," even the guilt of a dog who bit a man's hand depends on who the owner of the dog is — does it belong to the general, or is it a stray?; that is, on the circumstances surrounding the incident.

Such is the Russian worldview and mentality. It's not a matter of denying the law, but in setting the right priorities. A European will obey the law, no matter what it says, and sleep with the clear conscience of a law-abiding citizen. They will have absolutely no doubts. As for a Russian, even if they comply with an unfair - to their mind - rule of law, their conscience will not let them rest, nagging them for not acting according to the truth. With such a mentality, of course, there can be no rule of law in the Russian mind, because this is not how they think. We do not regard the law as the ultimate truth, hence the Russian proverb: 'The Law is like a drawbar: whichever way you turn it, there it goes.'

An interesting subject for serious cultural research involves comparing how Orthodoxy, Catholicism and Protestantism have influenced the formation of personality and the worldview in societies where they are or were dominant. In principle, we can already conclude it was Orthodoxy that did not permit the formation in the Russian consciousness of the idea of the impossibility of justice (truth) as a general idea, whereas Catholicism and Protestantism allowed such an idea to form. Democracy, which in the West means the equality of everyone before the law and the responsibility of everyone for their life and their role in society, is perceived as a free agent in Russia. 'I do as I please' — and I take no notice of the fact that I gradually stop identifying the country in which I live with myself. I stop believing that I can influence the situation in the country. Much of the population is focused on one single thought — how best to snatch their piece of the pie, and it's no holds barred, anything goes. The high-profile anti-corruption trials in Russia in recent years are a clear confirmation of this.

Democracy involves the personal participation of each citizen in the life of the state and assumes their personal responsibility for its present and future; that's how it works in the West. In Russia, we get the inverse of this — refusal to participate in the fate of this country. It's quite common to find that someone will furnish their apartment, fix it up, and then walk through a filthy lobby each day without thinking that it could and should be improved.

What's particularly interesting is that the difference in mentalities is not a trend of the last decade or even the last two or three decades. All this has long been ingrained in the consciousness of Western society, nurtured in law schools and penetrated the legal consciousness of the population. 'What? Justice? The law is the highest justice.' This is precisely what has been cultivated in Western society for many decades and even centuries, even in those historical periods when this society was still considered Christian and considered itself as such. There's your answer to the question of whose understanding of Christianity is closer to the Gospel and Christ.

THE RUSSIAN MENTALITY

The well-known Russian-American political scientist, Nikolai Zlobin wrote an interesting article in *Rossiyskaya Gazeta* on this topic. In it, he recounts a conversation he once had with a prominent American lawyer: 'As was common in those days, the conversation inevitably touched on the difference between Russia and America. We had already discussed history, politics, and economics, and then, inevitably, the conversation shifted to the difference in mentalities. The American began talking about the rule of law, and, in response, I began explaining to him how important a sense of justice is for people in Russia. He laughed and said: "In our law schools, as soon as a law student mentions justice as an argument on an exam, we immediately flunk him and make him retake the exam. Justice has got nothing to do with the functioning of the legal system. Its task is not to establish universal justice in the country, but to implement the principle of the rule of law as effectively as possible."' The reasoning here is that abstract justice doesn't exist — anywhere, ever. Justice is always context-specific, born of a certain historical moment in a specific social space. That which may seem like justice to one person or social group, may be a glaring injustice to another.

Reverence for the law and recognition of its supremacy in all matters is a distinguishing feature of an exemplary Western citizen. This is a fact that is frequently invoked to highlight the contrast to the Russian reality, or, more accurately, our generally acknowledged disregard for the law. 'The law is like a drawbar,' states a popular Russian proverb, as mentioned above. As every democratic human rights activist will tell you with a sigh, disrespect for the law is an inherent feature of Russian society. There is no tradition of respect for legal norms in despotic Russian society, which recognises only brute force and the authority of those in power.

For example, on August 12th 2018 the civil rights activist, Maxim Chikhunov appealed to the Russian Ministry of Internal Affairs to punish citizen, V. V. Putin for riding a motorcycle without a helmet in Sevastopol, and confirmed the violation with a corresponding video. In so doing, he probably did not expect that Putin would be punished. He wanted to use the expected rejection to underscore the pervasive lawlessness of Russian society.

The Ministry of Internal Affairs for Sevastopol, having considered the appeal of Maxim Chikhunov's lawyer refused to fine President Vladimir Putin for riding a motorcycle without a helmet during the festive protocol events in Sevastopol, Crimea, explaining that there are no grounds for bringing the head of state to justice. 'Road traffic is a set of social relations that arise in the process of moving people and goods with or without vehicles along roads... During various protocol events... there are no corresponding public relations, since traffic on road sections is completely eliminated,' stated the Ministry of Internal Affairs. 'In light of this, the traffic rules do not apply to persons and vehicles involved in such events.'

In his appeal, Chikhunov requested that Putin and the people accompanying him be punished under article 12.6 of the Administrative Code (violating the rules for using seat belts or motorcycle helmets) for riding a motorcycle without a helmet. The punishment for this offense is a fine of 1,000 roubles. In Europe, perhaps, this is exactly what would have happened. Therefore, there is a certain logic in the desire of the Russian liberal to break with this 'historical curse' and embark on the blessed European path. If we dig a little deeper, however, and try to figure out what is really going on here, we realise that the mentality of a classic Western citizen (which serves as the model for our particular civil rights activist) is a 'quiet horror' from the point of view of a citizen with a Russian mentality.

So, what's the matter here? What is our fundamental difference from Europeans and Americans, and why is it insurmountable without a radical break in the Russian character?

As we have already discovered, in the Western consciousness the concept of legality takes precedence over the concept of justice. The reasoning behind this seems perfectly acceptable — what is just for John may not be just for Bill. Therefore, there's no point in racking your brain over this justice of yours; the rule of law and its strict observance is the highest form of justice. Seem logical?

Herein lies the fundamental difference between the nature of a Russian and a Westerner; Russians are not in awe of the law. We do not prostrate ourselves before it and do not regard it as supreme. This is not because we are barbarians and are always trying to commit some crime or other, though; Russians have always seen something harsh and non-brotherly in the law. For Russians, the internal sense of justice and desire to live according to truth and conscience has always been above all laws. Today there is one ruler, one senate, one legislator, tomorrow another and the day after, a third. From the point of view of Western logic this is not a big deal as truth is relative, but for the Russian, who has accepted the commandments of Christ with the open heart of a child, such a vision of the world is unacceptable.

In his musings on the monarchy, Alexander Sergeyevich Pushkin expressed a rather interesting point of view. 'Why is it necessary that one of us be above others and even above the law? Why? Because the law is wood; in the law, a person hears something harsh and non-brotherly. Following the law to the letter won't get you very far; but none of us may break it or fail to abide by it; precisely for this, the highest Grace is needed, softening the law, which can appear to people only in one fully-fledged power. A state without a monarch is an automaton: all the more so if it achieves what the United States has achieved. What is the United States? A carcass; its people have weathered to the point of being completely worthless. A state without a fully-fledged monarch is like an orchestra without a conductor: no matter how good all the musicians are if there is none among them who will give a sign to everyone with the movement of a wand, the concert will come to nothing. It seems as if he himself doesn't do anything, doesn't play any instrument, only waves his wand lightly and looks at everyone, and just one glance is enough to soften, here and there, some rough sound that some fool would emit — a drum or awkward tulumbas. Under him, even the master's violin does not dare get too rowdy at the expense of others: he preserves the overall structure, gives life to the ensemble, and leads the supreme accord!'[38]

If the law does not ensure justice, does not serve the truth, then how can such a law be respected? For Russians, the law is a relative phenomenon. Today it is one thing, tomorrow, another, and if article 13 of the Basic Law states that state ideology is prohibited in Russia (and the majority of Russians do not share this point of view), then what should we do about this?

There is a demand for justice in our country. Just listen to all our conservative thinkers; they will tell you this is their most important demand. Justice in the eyes of the majority can only be established by the ruler, however, and except for a short period of judicial reform during the reign of Alexander II, there are not too many examples of justice being established by the court without regard for the possible negative reaction of the current government. The court does not yet enjoy indisputable authority in our society.

When asked in an interview by Vladimir Pozner whether he regards himself a European, the director, Andrei Konchalovsky replied that he doesn't. How is this possible, asked Pozner, after all, you have lived in America and Europe for many years? 'That's beside the point,' Konchalovsky replied. 'The thing is, in Europe they live by the laws, and I, like most Russians, live by ideas.'

When his dacha neighbours tried to complain about things such as where the ditch between the land plots should pass, one of my friends said 'go to court,' which, by his intonation could be taken as in that joke: 'go on a walking erotic tour with a sexual bias.'

---

[38] Spelling of A. S. Pushkin preserved.

THE RUSSIAN MENTALITY

Chapter 8 conclusions

In the Western mind, the concept of legality takes precedence over the concept of justice. The rule of law and its strict observance is the highest form of justice. Russians, though, are not in awe of the law and do not prostrate themselves before it, rather, we find something harsh and non-brotherly in the law, feeling that truth and conscience are above this. The powers that be change, but the word of the Lord is ever present.

There is a demand for justice in Russia, but this can only be established by the ruler, and there are not many examples of justice being established by the court without regard for the possible negative reaction of the current government, except for a short period of judicial reform during the reign of Alexander II. The court does not enjoy indisputable authority in our society. As stated by the director, Andrei Konchalovsky, Europeans live by the laws, whereas he, like most Russians, lives by ideas.

RUSSIAN MANAGEMENT

> *'A Russian is a person of two-sided actions:*
> *he can live both this way and in reverse,*
> *and in both cases he remains intact.'*
> A. Platonov. "Chevengur"

In 2001, the European businessman Manfred F. R. Kets de Vries, who had worked in Russia for several years, published a book entitled, *The Anarchist Within*. The book highlights a number of striking aspects of Russian culture and national character, helping us to better understand how various organisations function and how management processes are implemented. The author offers examples of his experiences in organisations in Russia.[39] Here are some quotes from the book:

'Russians are perceived as cold and harsh in their relations with outsiders; however, if a person is permitted into their personal space, they treat them very warmly. Russians establish deep friendships... The importance of friendship is also evident in the Russian approach to doing business.'

'If American and European managers are focused mainly on their task rather than on relations, then Russians, in order to successfully resolve business tasks, need to establish relationships. In everything Russians do, friendship is the most important thing.'

'Managing a structure (be it a separate commercial firm or a whole country) "by the rules" is almost impossible unless the rules begin to take on a life of their own, to "live a separate life." As a consequence, the number of loopholes increases as the rules are tightened or expanded.'

'Power has always been concentrated in the centre of Russia. As we

---

39 The Anarchist Within: Clinical Reflections on Russian Character and Leadership Style, Manfred F. R. Kets de Vries, Human Relations. 2001.

have seen, strong centralised leadership is regarded as a necessity, as a natural way to hold and structure a chaotic reality.'

'The Russian response to the fear of chaos, to the lack of checks and balances of power has always been centralised despotism. Russians hope that a paternalistic approach will ensure their security in a very insecure world.'

It would seem that during the years of his work in Russia, the author was able to get a sense of some of the nuances of Russian business mentality.

As we know, the third main type of Christianity, Protestantism, played a leading role in the formation of the bourgeois era, which opposed the ideology of private enterprise, personal initiative, and spiritual freedom in the class-feudal system (M. Weber).[40] In defining our management model, we should probably also take into account the fact that although it is a largely Orthodox country, Islam plays a significant role in Russia. In addition, it is important to remember that after the abolition of serfdom in 1861, by 1914 our country had become an industrial power. Though the emergence and development of capitalist relations did not always run smoothly, it should be noted there was no radical break in the consciousness of the population (especially as a state policy).

Looking at the system of governance since the formation of the Russian state, we can see that not everything in our country is done logically, and that management decisions often provoke justified criticism. At the same time, we have every reason to take pride in the achievements of those who have governed and managed our country, and who have successfully grappled with seemingly unsolvable challenges. For example:

The creation of combat-ready Red and White armies in the shortest possible time.

---

40   Maximilian Karl Emil Weber, known as Max Weber, was a German sociologist, philosopher, historian, and political economist. Weber's ideas have had a significant impact on the development of the social sciences, especially sociology.

The mass transfer of industry to the East at the outset of the Great Patriotic War, and the speedy restoration of the national economy after it ended; the creation of the space industry.

The creation of a 'nuclear shield;' the development and preservation in the 'roaring 90's' of a peaceful nuclear power industry which is a leading world player today, and many other achievements.

On the one hand, the Russian management model is obsessed with equalisation and virtually eliminates any competition; on the other, it somehow manages at critical moments to meet the challenges by promoting just the right people to key positions.

Many are aware that the work performed in our country could be done more efficiently and at a higher standard, and that our organisational skills could likewise use improvement; as for the state, this goes without saying. Russians are rather critical about the effectiveness of their leaders. However, this does not impede our assurance that our management system and our way of life as a whole have significant advantages. If we consider the results achieved, we will find that the end goals set by the country, the state or a large social group are usually achieved. 'The true defender of Russia is history: for three centuries, it has tirelessly worked to resolve in Russia's favour all the ordeals to which it subjects its mysterious fate,' in the words of the diplomat and poet, F. I. Tyutchev.

In some cases, success was achieved thanks to the state (territorial expansion and the authority of tsarist and Soviet Russia in foreign policy matters, the scientific achievements of the 1950s); in other cases, in spite of and even in opposition to it (for example, the flourishing of Russian classical literature in the XIX century). Regardless of which sphere we consider, we find the same pattern — inadequate and unsuitable means nonetheless achieve significant results. Apparently, herein lies the paradox: management which is inefficient at each specific point in time ultimately achieves a level of success which, in principle, should require effective management.

The military-political sphere is a good case in point: although, as a rule, Russia has had an outdated system of recruitment and army training, has lost many battles and even some wars, nevertheless, until recently, it has been acquiring territories rather than losing them.

The upsurge in science and education which took place in the USSR in the middle of the XX century is hard to explain. After all, these spheres were largely outside the public interest until the second half of the XIX century. Universities and academies appeared several centuries late in comparison to European countries, and for a long time, teachers and scientists had to be 'imported.' One would think that the Revolution and the consequent emigration of the most educated segments of the population and the country's isolation from the world community would have pushed science and education back. Instead, they made an impressive leap forward.

The same people within the framework of the same management system failed in cases that the system had prepared and planned for, and succeeded where they acted without a plan and preparation, with more freedom and independence at all levels of the management pyramid.

What is the main nerve of the Russian management system? What kind of relationship? These are measures to mobilise and allocate resources. Due to the fact that right from the outset a mechanism was built into the Russian governance system allowing it to mobilise, transfer and redistribute resources, the main role is played by those groups that mediate mobilisation and redistribution.[41]

In quiet times, the governance system functions in a stable mode and the managing apparatus, protecting itself from any manifestations of competition, tries to penetrate into the management of cluster cells (communities, platoons, brigades, collective farms, etc.). Any kind of initiative is suppressed, conventional schemes of work are imposed; the system degrades and becomes ineffective.

---

41   Prokhorov A. The Russian Management Model. Moscow: Art. Lebedev Studio Publishing House, 2011.

In times of crisis, the governance apparatus is seized by reformers and revolutionaries. The governance system goes into an emergency, unstable mode of operation; high-ranking authorities mobilise and redistribute resources, setting tough tasks. Forgetting the formal restrictions imposed upon them during the previous quiet period, those in the lower ranks act as they see fit to achieve their goals, and usually they succeed. Developed over the course of many centuries, 'cluster psychology,' the understanding that you can only survive and succeed together with your group, is that very same Russian 'collectivism' about which so much has been written and said. Therefore, it cannot be unequivocally stated that the centralisation of government has suppressed the initiative and independence of the Russian people. The forms taken by centralisation in Russia have helped preserve the stereotypes of the independent, autonomous behaviour of people; it's just that this autonomy has manifested itself in different ways during different phases of governance.

In the stable and stagnant phase, independence is manifested in the way people try to circumvent the law and various orders, how they avoid punishment and build their lives under the yoke of the state and the governance system. This is how they express their autonomy, creativity and initiative. In the unstable, emergency phase, independence is manifested in the proactive and unconventional ways the grassroots cluster units use to deal with the issues confronting them in this time of crisis.

Classical Western society is based on a competitive struggle between independent economic entities. In modern conditions, under the influence of state and public regulation, Western management systems are engaged in a kind of 'administration of competitors.' The state and society use non-competitive, largely administrative methods to regulate relations between economic, political and social units which compete with each other and within themselves: companies, religious denominations, scientific and artistic movements, political parties, and social movements.

Therefore, Western management can be called 'competitor administration.'

The Russian model in its unstable state does the exact opposite. It imposes competition between administrators on grassroots units and makes horizontal connections work. In Russia, within each cluster unit — in a workshop, on a team, in a company, in a military unit — relations are largely non-competitive, whereas between one another, the clusters are linked by competitive relations. This is a completely different type of activity — competition between administrators. This type of competition is significantly stronger than Western competition; it speeds up all processes, is infinitely more severe, and achieves greater power and competitive impact in a shorter period.

If in the Western management system, an army officer, for example, does not achieve the required result they lose in a competitive struggle with their colleagues, are not promoted or are dismissed or sent into early retirement. In Russia, during an unstable phase, an officer who headed a group which failed in a military operation may simply be court martialled and shot. Such an approach, as is commonly believed in Russia, provides a high rate of natural selection of capable managers.

At different times in history, the same characteristics of the management system are manifested in different ways. Thus, official career growth in Muscovite Rus was not a field of competition, since the correspondence of a position in the service was determined not by one's skills and abilities, but by gentility (the system of so-called parochialism). At the grassroots level among the peasantry, there was simply no question of any competition. The more hard-working and skilled peasants had no economic advantages over those who drank and were lazy, since the surplus product was taken away by the master and the state. The peasant community itself, with its inherent principle of mutual responsibility — when the one who could afford it paid for the one who could not - was another deterrent to competitive relations.

Serfdom, community, mutual responsibility and the fact that individual peasants could not own land are only the most obvious factors here. Orthodoxy, with its characteristic apology of equalisation and humility, also had an impact, and under the influence of these factors the mentality of the Russian people was formed. It's hardly surprising that competition was not destined to become the main driving force of Russia's economic development.

The ability of the management system to operate alternately in two modes, stable and emergency, initially contradicts the very idea of a rule-of-law state and a law-abiding population. If the same actions are perceived in fundamentally different ways depending on whether these actions are undertaken in a stable or unstable time, this contradicts the idea of the law and the rule of law. Therefore, the legal apparatus was forced to adapt to its own subordinate position and turn a blind eye to the fact that it will be violated right from the start. The law in this case exists in the form of a certain appendage which is valid for a limited period in relation to a limited range of issues.

If the Russian population were law-abiding, the Russian system of governance could not function; it would be impossible to move from an unstable state to a stable one and back, since it would be necessary to comply with a law focused on one particular state. The country has to choose either a rule-of-law state and a law-abiding population, or the possibility of switching from one mode of governance to another.

Having realised that embezzlement and bribery could not be dealt with by ordinary (legal) means, Peter I created special commissions of inquiry. Each consisted of guards officers — a major, a captain, a lieutenant - who were ordered to hear cases and judge not according to the law, but 'according to common sense and justice.'[42]

Accepting uncertainty as the norm of life, Russian managers em-

---

42   Klyuchevsky V. O. Collection of Works: In 8 volumes. The Course of Russian History. 1957. Vol. 4. P. 165

ploy in their activities the national habit developed over the centuries of having several standards of behaviour. For a Russian manager, it is in the order of things to simultaneously have certain rules in force as well as rules on how to break those same rules. This increases survival abilities in the most difficult conditions because the ability to live not in accordance with written instructions, the ability to adapt to the situation, is innovation, or, as they say now, creativity.

In Russia, there may be conditions where the old restrictions cease to apply and a completely new life begins. The combination of patience and impatience (in the sense of wanting to get results quickly) is a characteristic Russian trait. The competitive drive that has been suppressed for a long time bursts forth and rages no longer as civilised competition, but as a ruthless competition between administrators. The person whose character allows them to be both depending on the situation, is a true Russian. As the Russian writer, Leskov observed: 'We Russians are like cats — no matter where you throw us, we won't land with our faces in the dirt, we'll land on our paws — whatever the situation calls for, that's what we'll be, that's what we'll do: to die — then to die, to steal — then to steal.'

Main conclusions of Chapter 9

Looking at the system of governance since the formation of the Russian state, we can see that not everything in our country is done logically, and that management decisions often provoke justified criticism. At the same time, we can take pride in the achievements of those who have governed and managed our country and overcome seemingly insurmountable challenges.

Classical Western society is based on a competitive struggle between independent economic entities under state and public regulation: an 'administration of competitors.' The state and society use non-competitive, largely administrative methods to regulate relations between economic, political, and social units that compete with each other and within themselves. Therefore, Western management can be called 'competitor administration.'

The Russian management model in its unstable state does the opposite, imposing a 'competition between administrators' on each cluster unit. Within each unit, relations are largely non-competitive; instead, the clusters are linked by competitive relations: a competition between administrators. This type of competition is stronger than Western competition as it speeds up all processes, is more severe, and achieves a greater impact in a shorter period.

The ability of the management system to operate alternately in two modes, stable and emergency, initially contradicts the idea of a rule-of-law state and a law-abiding population, as the same actions are assessed in fundamentally different ways depending on the mode. Therefore, the Russian legal apparatus was forced to adapt to its subordinate position and exist as an appendage, which is valid for a limited period in relation to a limited range of issues.

If the Russian population were law-abiding, the Russian system of governance could not function as it would be impossible to move from an unstable state to a stable one and back, since it would be necessary to comply with a law focused on one particular state. The country has to choose between a rule-of-law state and the possibility of switching from one mode of governance to another.

Accepting uncertainty as the norm, Russian managers employ in their activities the national habit developed over the centuries of having several standards of behaviour. It is necessary to simultaneously have certain rules in force, as well as rules on how to break those rules. This increases survival abilities in the most adverse conditions through adaptability and innovation.

FREEDOM OF THE PRESS

Freedom of the press and freedom of speech are closely linked to questions about truth, governance, political flexibility, individual self-realisation, natural human rights and their protection.

Historically, they emerged as tools for ensuring awareness in civil society and maintaining a high level of competence in the state authorities. Thus, the English Bill of Rights of 1689[43] guaranteed to the Members of Parliament complete freedom to discuss the affairs of the kingdom and officials, without which its work would have been ineffective. This quality of freedom of speech is still valued even by certain authoritarian regimes, which leave small pockets of freedom that do not threaten their stability (for example, uncensored small-circulation newspapers) in order to have an objective idea of what is really happening in the region and beyond.

From a cultural point of view, freedom of speech affords one the possibility of developing one's own beliefs independently of society, and to formulate one's own standards and goals. Conversely, those who are endowed with these freedoms should use them wisely and for the benefit of society. Thus, people should not only have the freedom to discuss all public issues but also know how to use these freedoms to make informed choices.

Proponents of neoliberalism believe that freedom of speech depends on private property and the non-interference of the state in private business activities, including in the field of mass communications. In their view, not only does this serve as a barrier to state censorship, it also opens up additional opportunities for the spread of independent opinions. Conservatives who support state funding of the mass media (as well as election campaigns, education, etc.) take issue with this. They believe

---

43 Bill of Rights in Great Britain *a constitutional act*, the result of the Glorious Revolution of 1688–1689. Full title: An act proclaiming the rights and freedoms of subjects and establishing the order of inheritance of the crown.' Adopted on February 13th 1689 by a Parliamentary Convention.

that guaranteed support of the mass media is necessary for it to function independently of both public opinion and oligarchic money.

The purpose of this study is not to analyse the situation of the freedom of the press in Russia today. The aim is to discover how it is viewed by citizens with a Russian mentality and to consider some examples of freedom of the press in other countries.

Many in Russia find it incomprehensible that the "politically correct" West should tolerate rude and senseless insults against the Prophet Muhammad, as well as the Catholic Church. Why and what for? A person with a Russian mentality fails to see in the *Charlie Hebdo*[44] cartoons a manifestation of freedom of speech. They don't regard the desecration of religious symbols as a sign of civilisation. To their mind, such publications demonstrate disrespect and threaten to split society, provoking senseless conflicts. A large empire consisting of various ethnic groups cannot exist with such principles of freedom of speech as those demonstrated in *Charlie Hebdo*.

From a Western point of view, such publications confirm the existence of freedom of speech. It was largely to protect this freedom of speech that thousands of French citizens took to the streets of Paris after the terrorist attack against the publication's journalists in response to the scandalous (caricature of the Prophet Muhammad) publication. But how to explain this to those living in Russia?

In medieval Europe, anyone who insulted the king or committed an act of religious blasphemy was, as a rule, severely punished. For many years, Catholic England repressed all dissenters, but then Protestantism appeared and put pressure on the Catholics. History still preserves the bloody memory of those who were burned at the stake, the torture victims of religious and political conflicts. For example, several years after Martin Luther nailed his Ninety-Five Theses on a church door, German

---

[44] "Charlie Hebdo" is a French literary and artistic weekly magazine of political satire. It publishes cartoons, reports, discussions, and jokes of a nonconformist nature. Adopting left-wing and secular stances, it pokes fun at politicians, the far-right, Islam and Christianity.

peasants stood up against the aristocracy for their 'European freedom,' for which several hundred thousand rebels were mercilessly slaughtered.

A century later, the Thirty Years' War broke out in the Holy Roman Empire and the rest of Europe, in which millions of Protestants and Catholics butchered each other for their 'incorrect' interpretations of Christianity.

Subsequently, analysing its past, the West called these the 'Dark Ages,' and ushered in the period of the Enlightenment, or the Age of Reason. It was thanks to this historical path that liberal freedoms prevailed, granting independence from the Church and the king.

Based on this model, the mentality of today's Western civilisation, like that of the Parisian liberals who take pride in "Charlie" has formed. By insulting the Prophet of Islam, they demonstrate their cultural superiority to "primitive societies."

Many Brits love to read about the scabby details of the lives of their Royal family in the tabloids, whereas – until very recently - for Thais, the monarch has been sacred and to discuss him in negative terms was simply blasphemy. A Brit, regardless of their education and social status, can say anything they want about the Queen, so when they go to Thailand, their subconscious sees signs of the 'Dark Ages' and servile submissiveness in relation to the ruling dynasty.

When the liberal West heard the "Pussy Riot Prayer"[45] in Russia's main church, it was ecstatic. The technique used was clear: the "prayer" was spoken in the modern language of the West, in which such an act is a sign of freedom. The Western press was unanimous in its defence of the Pussy Riot's right to 'freedom of speech,' and, in the view of most Russian citizens, the right to behave like obnoxious brats before the entire country. The West is sure that punishing this group of girls for what they did

---

45   On February 19, 2012 at the Epiphany Chapel of the Epiphany Cathedral in Yelokhovo (Moscow) and on February 21 of the same year at the Cathedral of Christ the Saviour, members of the punk band Pussy Riot, held an event designated by the group as a "Punk Prayer 'Mother of God, send Putin away!'" The performance was filmed and edited, and the resulting video was posted on YouTube.

is unacceptable, since censoring their "performance" is a sign that Russia, with its sacred institutions, untouchable Patriarch and strong leader, remains in the 'Dark Ages.'

In Russia, however, there was no such dramatic division of the Middle Ages, the Renaissance and the Enlightenment. Even the October Revolution was more about daily bread and workers' conditions than freedom of speech. To this day, the Russian world remains uncertain about the correctness of its historical path. In the view of many, the 'period of godlessness' did much more harm than good. In Russia, you can discuss in all seriousness such topics as: 'Was the Revolution really necessary?' or 'Perhaps it would have been better not to break up the Soviet Union?' In the West, to declare: 'Perhaps it was better under an absolute monarchy?' — would, at the very least, mean making a fool of yourself. Such questions are not even discussed; only liberalism.

The idea of power as sacred[46] has been used in the West to repress the masses in the past, but in Russia, many would like to see this concept return and abolish the "wild freedoms" of the nineties. In their publication, the authors of *Charlie Hebdo* attempted to convey the absurdity of the 'Dark Ages' mentality, which 'still remains in the minds of the Arabs.' The Western world believes that, in so doing, not only does it demonstrate its freedom but also offers a lesson in civility to others. For Muslims and the Russian world, however, this argument in favour of the civility of liberal Europe doesn't look too impressive.

Vladimir Pozner, a well-known Russian liberal journalist who has lived and worked in America for a long time, has said a lot of interesting things about freedom of speech in the United States. One interesting story involves the NBC journalist, Jon Alpert, who was fired for uncoordinated coverage of the first American military operation in Iraq: 'In 1991, during the first Iraq war, called "Desert Storm," a very famous journalist,

---

[46] Sacred — in a broad sense, related to the divine, the mystical. Something material, but located above ordinary things, concepts, phenomena. At the same time also spiritual, irrational, and unknowable.

THE RUSSIAN MENTALITY

Jon Alpert, as a stringer on NBC[47] offered to go behind the front lines. Let me remind you that no journalist, American or foreign, was allowed to get information from sources other than the American military leadership in Iraq. Jon Alpert suggested circumventing this rule, and the executive producer of NBC News at the time gave him permission to do so.

'Alpert was able to film what was happening in Iraqi cities. As it turned out, the so-called smart bombs are not all smart, not all of them fall neatly on military targets, and sometimes women, children and the elderly are killed. And he showed the NBC management these people, showed their relatives crying, showed the ruins of residential buildings.

'As a consequence, he wasn't simply fired. He was blacklisted.'

On February 28th 2003, American TV host Phil Donahue was fired. For six months prior to that, Donahue had hosted a daily political talk show on NBC. Supposedly, the programme failed to meet the expectations of the management, and they decided to part ways with the famous presenter. Here's how Donahue's former colleague and co-host, Russian journalist Vladimir Pozner describes it: 'Now Donahue tells me about what happened as almost a kind of joke. He said, "You know, I'm learning political science. Now we are falling back to the 50s, when people are required to swear an oath of allegiance. You must be a patriot; you can't object to the war in Iraq. If you object, this is how it ends." In their official statement, Donahue and his team said that the programme on the cable channel he worked for, NBC, had the highest rating of any primetime programme on that channel. In other words, exactly the opposite — the programme had high ratings, but the management found the content very disturbing because it was not patriotic.'

In Pozner's view, expressed in 2003, the situation as regards freedom of speech was better in Russia than in the United States: 'Today, in America, you can't take issue with what the White House says without

---

47 Freelance journalist, reporting and filming from hot spots.

suffering negative consequences, for instance, losing your job on television. And I will say something that may come as a surprise to many. I am absolutely convinced that today in Russia there is much more freedom of speech: we can criticise the President, the war in Chechnya, and so on, much more than in America, where even a famous TV host like Donahue can't criticise the White House war in Iraq.'

Main conclusions of Chapter 10

The state of freedom of the press in Russia today is assessed very negatively by Western countries. In their view, although opposition media does exist, it is under strong pressure by the authorities.

Those who are endowed with the power of freedom of speech should use it wisely and for the benefit of society to make informed choices. The majority of the population in Russia today has confidence in the government, which is confirmed by numerous public opinion polls, including agencies with a liberal orientation. However, in the view of the opposition, the government does not give the 'morally leading minority' a chance to speak out without restrictions.

Today, in 2020, half of America is slinging mud at its President and his policies, even going so far as to conjure up lies and falsifications. In this regard, the White House gives as good as it gets in relation to its opponents. The whole world understands that two oligarchic groups are using the forces of "independent, unbiased" journalists to wage war on each other. Is this the much coveted right to freedom of speech?

RUSSOPHOBIA AND NATIONALOPHOBIA

External and internal Russophobia

In his time, the Russian philosopher I. A. Ilyin, enumerating the characteristic features of the West's attitude to Russia in the XIX century, found in Europe a whole 'nest of bad affects: fear, arrogance, hostility, envy and ignorant slander.' Ilyin's succinct, precise and expressive formula, which explains the essence of this attitude, boils down to the following: 'The Europeans need Russia "barbaric" in order to "civilise" her unto their manner; threatening in its size, to split her up; aggressive, to organise a coalition against her; reactionary, to justify a revolution in her and demand a republic for her; undergoing religious decay, to break into her with Reformation or Catholic propaganda; economically untenable, to claim her "unused" space, her raw materials, or to at least score some lucrative trade agreements and concessions. But if this "rotten" Russia can be used strategically, then the Europeans are ready to form alliances with her and demand military efforts from her "to the last drop of its blood."'[48] Basically, Ilyin has laid out the outlines of external Russophobia.

It is generally held that the term 'Russophobia' was first introduced into public circulation by F. I. Tyutchev, who pointed out that the basis of Russophobia is hatred, a raging, blind, violent, hostile sentiment towards Russia.

Western-oriented Russian liberals, who live both in Europe and in Russia are people who have no national sense whatsoever, and whose Russophobia, according to Tyutchev, is instinctive, unprincipled, not based on logic, and is generally irrational.[49]

---

48   Ilyin I. A. The World Politics of Russian Sovereigns // Professor I. A. Ilyin. Our tasks. Articles 1948–1954. Volume I. Paris: Publication of the Russian General Military Union, 1956.

49   Tyutchev F. I. Letters to Moscow publicists. I. S. and A. F. Aksakov. 18611872.27. A. F. Aksakova. Petersburg. Wednesday, 20 September [1867] // Literary Heritage. Vol. 97. Fyodor Ivanovich Tyutchev. Book one. M., 1988.

As we can see, there are two types of Russophobia — 'external' and 'internal.' As an example of the modern ideological basis of external Russophobia, we will choose the book, *Russia Under the Old Regime*, by R. Pipes, first published in 1974, which comes particularly close to our line of inquiry in its main conclusions.[50]

The subject of the book is Russia's political system. It traces the growth of Russian statehood from its inception in the IX century to the end of the XIX century, and the parallel development of the main estates — the peasantry, the nobility, the middle class and the clergy. It raises the following question: why in Russia, in contrast to the rest of Europe, to which Russia belongs by virtue of its geographical location, race and faith, was society unable to impose any serious limitations on political authority? The author offers several answers to this question and tries to show how opposition to absolutism in Russia tended to take the form of a struggle for various ideals rather than class interests, and how the tsarist government, in response to the corresponding attacks, developed administrative methods that clearly anticipated the methods of the modern police state. Unlike most historians, who look for the roots of twentieth-century totalitarianism in Western ideas, Pipes seeks them in Russia's institutions. In particular, the author underscores the relationship between personal property and political power.

In a primitive society, power over people is combined with power over things, and it took an extremely complex evolution of law and institutions (beginning in Ancient Rome) for it to split into power manifested as sovereignty and power as property. According to Pipes, in Russia, this split happened very late and took a rather flawed form. Russia belongs to the category of states that political and social scientists refer to as 'patrimonial.' In such states, political power is conceived and manifested as a continuation of legal ownership, and the ruler is both the sovereign of the state and its owner. The difficulties associated with maintaining this

---

50   Richard Pipes: Russia Under the Old Regime. — M.: Zakharov, 2012.

THE RUSSIAN MENTALITY

type of regime in the face of ever-increasing contacts and rivalry with the West, which has a different system of government, has created a state of permanent internal tension in Russia (including severe suppression of dissent), which has not been overcome to this day.

Pipes asks why Russia needed a large and modern army at the end of the XVII century, taking into account that it was already the largest country in the world and strategically one of the least vulnerable (as noted above, the available troops were quite enough to defend its sprawling eastern and southern borders).

He rejects the explanation of Russian historians that Russia needed a powerful modern army to solve the so-called 'national tasks' of ensuring the country's security. According to Pipes, history demonstrates that the solution of these problems during the XVIII century did not satisfy Russia's territorial appetites. Having acquired during the partitions of Poland territory that it regarded as its legitimate fiefdom, Russia then absorbed in 1815 the Kingdom of Warsaw, which it had never owned, and even made claims to Saxony. No sooner had it taken possession of the northern coast of the Black Sea and its ice-free ports, than it laid claim to its southern coast with Constantinople and the straits. Having gained access to the Baltic Sea, it captured Finland. One can always justify new conquests by the need to defend old ones — this is the usual justification for any form of imperialism.

The logical conclusion of this type of thinking, in Pipes' opinion, is conquest on a global scale, since this is the only way this state could guarantee that its possessions were completely protected from external threats.

Thus, Richard Pipes (1923–2018), professor at Harvard University, long-term director of the Russian Research Center there and advisor to American presidents, created an ideological basis for Russophobia, and justified the potential danger to democratic countries posed by Russia, which Western politicians actively use.

On the heels of Pipes' book, a series of articles in a similar spirit appeared in the 1980s in magazines founded in the West by recent Soviet immigrants.[51] These publications may quite reasonably be regarded as a manifestation of 'internal' or 'Russian Russophobia.'

Here is a very condensed summary of the main points made in these publications:

The history of Russia beginning in the early Middle Ages is defined by certain 'archetypal' Russian traits: a slavish mentality, lack of self-esteem, intolerance towards the opinions of others, a lackey's mixture of anger, envy and worship of those in power.

Since times immemorial, Russians have loved strong, cruel power, and its very cruelty; throughout their entire history, they have been predisposed to slavishly submit to force, and to this day the psyche of the people is dominated by a 'longing for a Master.'

In parallel, Russian history since the XV century has been permeated by dreams of Russia's role or mission in the world, a desire to teach others something, to point out a new path or even save the world. This is 'Russian Messianism' (or, simply put, 'universal Russian arrogance'), the origins of which the authors trace back to the concept of 'Moscow — the Third Rome,' expressed in the XVI century, and in its current stage in the idea of a global Socialist revolution, initiated by Russia.

As a consequence, Russia constantly finds itself at the mercy of despotic regimes and bloody catastrophes, such as the eras of Ivan the Terrible, Peter I, and Stalin.

Russians are unable to understand the reason for their misfortunes. They react with suspicion and hostility to anything foreign, and always try to find someone else to blame for their troubles: the Tatars, Greeks, Germans, Jews… just as long as it's not their fault.

---

51   Magazines: "Syntax" (Paris), "Time and We" (tel Aviv), "Continent" (Paris), European magazines and newspapers. — 1975–1990 Authors: Shragin, Pomerants, Amalrik, Gorsky (pseudonym).

THE RUSSIAN MENTALITY

The Revolution of 1917 follows logically from the whole of Russian history. In essence, it wasn't Marxist at all; the Russians subverted Marxism and used it to restore the Russian tradition of strong power. The brutalities of the Revolution and the Stalinist period follow naturally from the specificities of the national character. Stalin was a characteristically national, very Russian phenomenon, and his policy was a direct continuation of Russia's barbaric history. Stalinism can be traced back at least four centuries in Russian history.

We can see the same trend continuing to this day. Freeing itself from an alien and incomprehensible Europeanised culture, the country is becoming more and more like Muscovite Rus.

The greatest danger hanging over Russia right now is its resurgent attempts to find some kind of unique path of its own development — a manifestation of that centuries-old 'Russian Messianism.' Such an attempt will inevitably lead to a rise of Russian nationalism, a resurgence of Stalinism, and a wave of anti-Semitism. It poses a grave danger not only for the peoples of the former USSR, but for humanity as a whole. The only hope lies in understanding the destructive nature of these trends, eradicating them, and building a society based exactly on the model of modern Western democracies.

Some Russian Russophobes express an uncompromisingly pessimistic point of view, excluding the hope of any meaningful existence for Russia. There was never any history, there was only a 'being outside of history;' the people turned out to be an imaginary quantity, the Russians only demonstrated their historical impotence, and Russia is doomed to collapse and destruction.

The argument put forth by many authors about the 'slavish' Russian soul, that Russians have a less developed sense of self-respect and personal dignity than Westerners is difficult to support with any facts. Alexander Pushkin, for example, believed that the ratio is the opposite. The opinions of foreign visitors, who saw Russia as a country of Asiatic despotism and its inhabitants as slaves, can be contrasted with the views of other foreigners who were amazed by the sense of personal dignity displayed by the Russian peasant, even seeing in Russia 'an ideal country, full of honesty and simplicity.' In all likelihood, both groups knew very little about the real Russia.

The attitude towards power in Muscovite Rus does not resemble 'slavish submission' in any way. The term 'autocrat,' which was included in the title of the Russian tsar, did not mean recognition of his right to arbitrariness and irresponsibility, but only expressed that he was a sovereign and not a tributary of anyone (specifically, the khan). According to the views of the time, the tsar was responsible to God and had to uphold religious and moral norms, as a tsar who violated these duties should not be obeyed, even if this entailed torment and death. A stark example of the condemnation of a tsar is the assessment of Ivan the Terrible, not only in chronicles but also folk legends; in one of them, for instance, we find the view that the 'Tsar deceived God.' Similarly, Peter I was known as the 'Antichrist' among the people, and Alexey as a martyr for the faith.

How little the attitude of Russians to power prior to the era of Peter I resembled slavish submission is demonstrated by the Great Schism: when minor changes introduced by the authorities to rites that did not have dogmatic significance were not accepted by much of the nation, people fled by the thousands to forests, willingly suffered torment and setting themselves on fire — and for 300 years the issue did not wane in its relevance.[52]

The active leader of that time, Archpriest Avvakum Petrov is an immense figure. This is a unique case when one person simultaneously reflected the era that demarcated deeply religious medieval Russia and a new secular state with a different type of culture and political structure.

---

52   Shafarevich I. R. Essays in three volumes. Vol. 2. — M.: Phoenix, 1994.

In his early twenties, Avvakum was ordained a deacon, and shortly thereafter, in 1644 he was ordained a priest and given his own parish – nothing to make him stand out from hundreds of similar priests. Later, however, Avvakum became a guiding light for many people by following the life path of Jesus Christ, imitating his passions and sufferings, his parables, love for his disciples and severity to the Pharisees.

The defenders of antiquity courageously reformed reality - just as the leaders of the European Reformation did - raising the ideal of early Christianity above everyday life and concessions to human frailties. The unyielding reformist spirit was strong in them. It is no accident that the leading industrialists of Russia in the XVIII–XIX centuries — bold economic reformers — emerged from the conservative Old Believers: merchants and entrepreneurs, often former peasants, who retained their moral principles and firm faith even after becoming millionaires.

What is most striking is that Avvakum introduced into Russian culture an example of a person able to overcome obstacles. In his freedom of thought and speech was the harbinger of a new secular culture which challenged both the conservative foundations of society and bureaucratic depersonalisation. Avvakum offered people a new kind of role model, not of a rebel trying to bring about change by force, but that of a deep thinker with mature freedom of conscience who was ready to pay for his beliefs with his life.[53]

The idea of 'Moscow — the Third Rome,' formulated at the beginning of the XVI century by the Pskov monk Philotheus, reflected the historical situation of the time. After the Florentine union of Byzantium and Catholicism and the fall of Constantinople, Russia remained the only Orthodox kingdom, and Philotheus urged the tsar to grasp his responsibility in this new situation. He reminded him of what befell the First and the Second Rome (Constantinople), which died, in his view, because the

---

53   O. Chumicheva. The Project "Arzamas. The History of Russian Culture. Muscovite Rus". 2018. Lecture 6. URL: https://www.liveinternet.ru

true faith was not kept, and predicted that Russia would stand forever only if it remained true to Orthodoxy. This theory was in no way political and did not push Russia towards any expansion or Orthodox missionary work, nor was it reflected in any way in the popular consciousness (in folklore, for instance). The claim that the idea of a 'Third Rome' and the revolutionary Marxist ideology of the XX century form a single tradition belongs to Berdyaev, who seems to have been particularly captivated by the concord of the Third Rome with the Third International. He made no attempt, however, to explain how this concept existed for 400 years without in any way manifesting itself during this time.

Though purity of the faith was a huge concern and Protestant and Catholic missionary activities aroused suspicion, there is no evidence of any specifically Russian hatred of foreigners and foreign influences that would distinguish them from other peoples. A certain religious intolerance is evident here, but this feature does not distinguish Russia at that time from the West, where levels of religious tolerance were characterised by the Inquisition, the St. Bartholomew's Day Massacre and the Thirty Years' War. Thus, many of the phenomena that Russophobe authors attribute are not only not typical for Russia but non-Russian in origin; imports from the West, they are a kind of payment for Russia's entry into the sphere of the new Western culture. Such arguments abound, but it is probably enough to give this assessment of the concept under discussion: it simply falls apart under scrutiny. The views presented mainly focus on two arguments: that the Russian national principle poses a danger to the life of the state and must therefore not be allowed to influence it, and that in building a society, modern Western democracies must strictly be used as a model. The authors are very touchy about any attempts to approach today's problems from the point of view of Russian spiritual and historical traditions.

THE RUSSIAN MENTALITY

'Not national rebirth, but the struggle for freedom and spiritual values should become the central creative idea of our future,' wrote Yuriy Horodyanin-Lisovsky under the pseudonym. Gorsky. 'The new national consciousness must not be built on unconscious patriotism,' (as, apparently, it was built by the 20 million who laid down their lives for our victory in the Great Patriotic War).

The opinion that 'Russia has no history' might be dismissed as a polemical exaggeration, but essentially the views of all these Russophobes lead to this conclusion: History, as that womb in which the future of the people is nurtured, Russia, according to their point of view, did not have. On what, then, is the future of this country to be built?' The answer can be found in the second main thesis put forth in the literature under consideration: based on someone else's experience; by taking modern Western multi-party democracy as the model. It is the fact that this is someone else's experience, that it has not grown organically from Russian history that makes it attractive, since this serves as a guarantee it is not infected with the poisons that, according to the authors, permeate our past. Thus, in effect, it is the search for one's own path (of course, without limiting its direction, so the result could be some kind of democracy of one's own) that is rejected here. The reason, according to the authors, is that only two possible solutions exist and a choice must be made between them: modern Western-style democracy or totalitarianism.

The past several years have seen an intensification in the activities of the 'Westernist' movement aimed at destroying the true ontological foundations of Russian culture as a whole. It's disturbing to note, for example, the increasing criticism the Cyrillic alphabet is getting in the press. The need to transliterate it into the supposedly "most perfect alphabet in the world" (the Latin script) is justified by the goals of the all-encompassing civilisational processes of globalisation. If Russia wants to keep up with the progressive world, proponents of this reform maintain, if it wants to be part of Europe, then it must completely switch to the Latin alphabet, and sooner or later it will realise this and do so. As the writer, V. Rasputin says, however: 'Let's hope that… the Cyrillic alphabet will not be abandoned after all. This would amount to an ultimate suicide for the nation. Just imagine reading *The Tale about Igor's Campaign* and *The Sermon on Law and Grace*, Pushkin and Gogol, Dostoevsky and Tolstoy, Tyutchev and Yesenin in Latin! Or translating into Latin Vanka Zhukov's letter to his grandfather's village, and the letters of our fathers and grandfathers from the frontlines of the Great Patriotic War! Abandoning the Orthodox faith and all our cultural and spiritual heritage! No, this is simply inconceivable.'

As for Western-style democracy, which the authors in question insistently present as a universal solution to all social problems, in its current state it raises a number of doubts which should be carefully discussed before recommending its unconditional acceptance as the only solution to our problems. Let's take a look at some of them.

Firstly, the transition to this order is not as straightforward as one might think. Usually, the path to it involves bloodshed and suffering; obviously, some kind of violence is necessary when you try to interfere with the natural historical process. Such was the case with the Civil War in England, whilst in France the Civil War and the Terror were just the beginning. For nearly a century afterwards, the country was rattled by convulsions: the Napoleonic wars, the revolutions, the Second Empire and the Commune. Our attempt to introduce this order in February 1917 did not meet with success. In Germany, this attempt, carried out in the Weimar Republic, resulted in the victory of National Socialism as a reaction. (In his memoirs, Churchill suggests that the fate of Germany would have been different if the monarchy had been preserved in 1918.)

Can we now risk another such disaster in our country? Is there any chance that it would survive it? The Westernists recommend this path with such ease that it makes one suspect they are not bothered by these concerns in the least.

For the past 30 years, the dialogue between the intelligentsia and the people has consistently resembled the all-too-familiar monologue in Russian history — the intelligentsia speaks whilst the people mainly keep quiet. It should be noted that to 'keep quiet' does not mean complete silence, however, as from time to time they do speak out.

It must be said that this dialogue between the intelligentsia and the people has always been a strange construction, since from the outset the intention of Russian cultural figures was to speak not to the people, but about the people. Today, the liberal intelligentsia are especially passionate about 'shaking the dust of the people off their feet.' The argument that history is shaped by the active five percent of the population with an ultra-liberal ideology has become very popular. The world stage is once again being dominated by those whose aim is not to bring joy to the people through social justice, but to eliminate the people from the audience altogether. In their view, the Russian people play only a negative role — they are a moral freak on the stage of world history, unable to organise themselves and offending the fragile and vulnerable intellectual who wishes them nothing but good.

Civil war is the normal state of Russian society. This opinion was voiced on December 25th 2018 by the poet, Dmitry Bykov at the Amateur Readings in St. Petersburg. The poet's speech was published by the Nevex.TV channel. 'Do you think that Putin's power will now collapse and that Russia will become free? Nothing doing. A mutual extermination will take place, and quite an intense one. The only thing holding us back now is some semblance of illusory power. Every revolution in Russia ends in a civil war,' he stated. Revolutions in Russia are usually followed by 'troubled times,' the poet added. 'Until Russia is split up into several states, it will enter the stage of civil war. This is by no means an appeal.

This is not separatism… Unfortunately, Russia has, as they say, already been there and done that: every revolution ends in a civil war, every civil war ends in terror. Such is the country: it is improperly organised.'

As the journalist, Valery Panyushkin[54] says, 'it would be easier for everyone in the world if the Russian nation came to an end. The Russians themselves would be much relieved if tomorrow they no longer had to form a national state, but could turn into a small people, such as the Vods, Khants, or Avars.'

Internal Russophobia most often expresses itself through negative feelings, but also usually demands that Russia be destroyed. For example, the music critic, Artemy Troitsky is rather fond of commenting on this topic: 'I regard Russian men, for the most part, as animals, creatures not even of a second, but of a third-class. When I see them, beginning with cops and ending with political officials, I believe that they, in principle, should become extinct. Fortunately, they are successfully working on precisely this as we speak. I hate the Russian state, have always hated it, and will continue to hate it… The best thing for this country would be to sell it, piece by piece, to those who will offer the most for it.'

Another outspoken Russophobe is Yuri Nesterenko, who received political asylum in the United States in 2011. His is a kind of sad resignation: if you can't destroy Russia, then you must at least eliminate it from your life. The well-known text of the article, "Exodus" has so encapsulated all the main aforementioned ideologies of Russophobia that we will give extensive quotes from it here.

'Russia is evil. Russia is evil incarnate, in its pure form.' This quality of Russia is determined by its people, who are unworthy of human status: 'The same people, and if you call a spade a spade — a slavish and servile biomass which has supported, nourished and regularly generated them

---

54   Valery Panyushkin, worked for the Russian magazine The New Times, "Vedomosti" newspaper, and "Snob" magazine. He hosted his own show on the "Dozhd" channel, and served as editor-in-chief of the "Such Things" information portal. Since April 2018 he has been the editor-in-chief of Rusfond. Awards: Gratitude of the President of the Russian Federation (April 28, 2012) — *'for active charitable and social activities.'*

over the course of eight centuries… Russia as a state… was generated, on the one hand, by the Horde of Asian conquerors, and on the other hand, by the Moscow prince-traitors… collaborators serving the Horde… who passed along all the worst qualities of the Horde tradition to a country united by blood and meanness…. During the course of all these centuries, Russia has not only not corrected anything, it has only made the situation worse, developing, strengthening and elevating all the most disgusting tendencies and vices to the level of pride.'

What follows is a declaration of Russia's hopelessness, supplemented by statements about Russian hatred of freedom and desire for Empire: 'The thing is, Russia is a hopeless swamp in which any and all bright and progressive initiatives get bogged down. It is a country whose people - with rare exceptions - feel a sincere hatred and aversion to freedom, and - contrary to Marx's thesis, first of all - to their own, and only then and as a result, to others. A people who deeply despise self-esteem, intelligence ('Well, the Smart Aleck just couldn't keep his mouth shut!'), and individuality, who hate anyone who stands out above mediocrity… Who regards the very desire to live independently and in prosperity as a vice, and who sees virtue in, respectively, a mindless herd mentality and subservience, a willingness to live in shit and filth… and, with no second thoughts, to sacrifice themselves in the name of a small herd — community, and a large herd — Empire. A people who in all sincerity adore tyrants (both their own and those of others). A people not merely of slaves, as even slaves may still dream of freedom at times, but precisely lackeys who dream only of a good master — and "good" here means not kind, but exactly the opposite — one able to inspire fear both in neighbours and in their own… Eight centuries of bloody bestiality and stupid meanness, eighteen failed attempts at modernisation — is it not enough? The time has come to acknowledge the obvious truth: this country and these people are hopeless.'

The emergence and development of nationalophobia

A phobia implies a persistent fear and hatred of its source, and it is unlikely that there are neighbouring peoples who have never experienced such feelings for one another. Here we come to the first and very important question: is Russophobia an instance of one such typical case, or is it a completely ordinary phenomenon, all the more natural since such a large and influential people as the Russians have had many confrontational relations with other peoples in history? In his time, Ilyin made such an assumption: 'Just as there are "Anglophobes," "Germanophobes," "Japanophobes," so the world is full of "Russophobes," those who hate Russia and believe that its collapse, humiliation and weakening will bring them unbridled success.'

In this light, Russophobia appears as a completely banal phenomenon, and perhaps we shouldn't regard every hostile response or attack on the Russian people as Russophobia. Russophobia is not simply a dislike of Russia, and certainly not just any criticism, however; it is a conscious hatred of those who possess the Russian mentality and, as a consequence, of Russian statehood.

For example, Anglophobia arose among continental European peoples in reaction to the calculating and at times exploitative policies of the British ruling elites, whose goal was to take over new lands and assimilate or enslave the indigenous peoples. The disrespect of the British to the language and culture of these indigenous peoples, as well as their overt demonstrations of racism and segregationist policies contributed to the emergence of Anglophobia as a political phenomenon.

Anglophobia in the XIX century was also widespread in Russia. The famous writer, Prince V. F. Odoevsky, believed that the history of England served as a lesson to people who 'sell their souls for money;' that its present was sad and its death inevitable. The historian, writer and journalist, M. P. Pogodin called the Bank of England the golden heart of England, as it was 'unlikely to have another one.' Professor at the Moscow State University, literary critic and literary historian, S. P. Shevyrev commented: 'It erected not a spiritual idol, like others, but a golden calf before all nations and for this it will one day answer to the justice of heaven.' The journal, *Notes of the Fatherland*, meanwhile, remarked that British scientists and writers 'work for the benefit of the flesh, not the soul.' In the press, Great Britain has been referred to as the 'Treacherous Albion,' 'Decrepit Albion,' and the 'Metropolis of gold.'

Anglophobia in France has a long tradition with explicitly anti-globalist connotations which dates back to the beginning of the Hundred Years' War. It became more entrenched after the incident at Mer el-Kabir on July 3rd 1940, when British ships sank the entire French fleet killing thousands of sailors whilst the French admiral was considering a British proposal. A few years later, the Vichy journalist, Jean Herold-Paquis, began attaching to the end of his statements the call: 'England, just like Carthage, must be destroyed.'

Meanwhile, in America, Francophobia intensified when France led a group of countries at the UN that opposed military action in Iraq, leading to a pronounced cooling in US-French relations. The position taken by France at the UN Security Council caused a wave of Francophobia in the United States. Cultural differences between the French and the Americans are nothing new. Accusations of arrogance from both sides are commonplace, but at that time anti-French sentiment in the United States took a more serious turn.

The tabloid *New York Post* ran a front-page photo showing the French and German representatives at the United Nations. Instead of human heads, however, they had the heads of weasels, animals which are associated with treachery and cowardice in America. The hosts of pop music radio programmes in Atlanta gave their listeners the opportunity to smash a French Peugeot car with a sledgehammer. Almost every night on TV, the hosts of late-night comedy shows poked fun at the French, with jokes such as, 'Going to war without the French is like going hunting without an accordion.'

Missouri congressman Roy Blunt launched the Republican caucus meeting with the question: 'How many Frenchmen does it take to protect Paris from its enemies?' After a brief pause for effect, Blunt said that the answer is unknown, since this has never happened. Two Republican congressmen persuaded their colleagues to change the name of 'French fries' on the House cafeteria menu to 'Freedom fries,' and the name of 'French toast' to 'freedom toast.'

The French hotel company, Sofitel, replaced the French flag at the entrance to its branches in ten US cities with the American flag or a city flag. The popular political TV show host, Bill O'Reilly urged his viewers to boycott French goods. One of those who took up O'Reilly's call — Ken Wagner, the owner of a popular restaurant in the Florida city of West Palm Beach — poured the contents of all the French wine he had in stock into a sewer, saying: 'It seems the French have forgotten what happened in Normandy during the Second World War and in the Argonne Forest during the First. Have they forgotten our Marshall plan, which helped revive Europe?'

Undoubtedly, the spread of American values impacts the national characteristics of countries which are affected by its history and traditions. The influence of American values tends to lead to a standardisation of lifestyle, imposing a uniform culture dominated by values inherent in America. Unsurprisingly, this process provokes the indignation and discontent of large numbers of people in different countries around the world, since the ethnic, cultural, and civilisational diversity of the world is the wealth of humanity and serves as a source of its spiritual development.

THE RUSSIAN MENTALITY

Americanophobia, or anti-Americanism, has received a great deal of academic attention. In this century alone, about a hundred academic studies have been published abroad exploring the origins and causes of hatred towards Americans by the Germans, French, Dutch, Mexicans, Italians, Australians, Filipinos, Portuguese, Chinese, Vietnamese, Cubans and others. In the US, there is even a fund dedicated to this phenomenon: the Pew Research Center. Each year, it allocates money globally to investigate why Americans are so disliked, as Americans must stay informed about this factor which impacts their income in such a significant way.

The same cannot be said about Russophobia. No research exists on this subject. Mostly you will hear that all this Russophobia stuff is a figment of their imaginations, a product of their complexes, and if Russians behaved in a civilised manner, like the Americans or Europeans, no one would criticise them and they would be accepted into the friendly European family with open arms. But the Russians don't understand this. As A. Venediktov, the editor-in-chief of the *Echo of Moscow* radio station put it during a broadcast: 'When they start getting carried away and showing everyone Kuzma's mother, this is when Russophobia begins in the world... As soon as we get it into our heads to teach everyone how to live properly — be it in Nikolayev's time or in the era of Alexander III, it makes no difference — then the world begins to look askance at us and Russophobia develops, followed closely by a coalition against Russia.'

Main conclusions of Chapter 11

What can we say in answer to internal Russophobes? One enters this world and departs from it, as a rule, among their own people. Belonging to a specific cultural group makes one a part of history, the mysteries of the past and the future. One is able to sense (at a subconscious level, most often) the significance and higher meaning of humanity's earthly existence and one's role in it. History may be regarded as a two-way process of mutual influence between an individual and their social environment — their people. We have seen what the individual gets from belonging to this social group. The individual, in turn, creates the forces that hold the people together and ensures their existence: language, folklore, art, and awareness of their historical destiny. When this two-way process breaks down, the same thing happens as in nature: the environment dies.

Taking all this into account, we simply haven't got the right to permit the desire for an understanding of our national path to be slandered, trampled on and perverted. We must protect our national consciousness from the complex of doom being imposed on us and the belief that our people are useful only as material for the experiments of others.

THE RUSSIAN MENTALITY

PROBLEMS HINDERING THE RUSSIAN ECONOMY FROM OCCUPYING A WORTHY PLACE IN THE WORLD: CORRUPTION, BUREAUCRACY, NEPOTISM, AS A PERSONNEL POLICY...

Corruption

Let's take the problem of corruption, which unfortunately is widespread in Russia and prevalent on an unprecedented scale. It is believed that it is one of the characteristic features of our mentality dating back to the times of empire. Evidence of this can be found in the remarkable work of the merchant-tax farmer, V. Kokorev, *Failings in the Russian Economy*, published in the 1860s.

How to combat corruption is one of the eternal issues in organising a state. Regarding corruption as a systemic phenomenon, the Russian state has been creating and implementing comprehensive measures to counter it. Since 2008, the Anti-Corruption Council under the President of the Russian Federation has been formed, national anti-corruption plans developed and approved, a package of anti-corruption laws passed, and a number of presidential decrees have extended control over the activities of state and municipal employees and heads of state corporations.[55]

Specific measures which can reduce corruption in the state and society and identify and punish those involved play an important role in the fight against corruption. A fairly simple and effective measure is the mandatory annual reporting of officials (officials of executive authorities and deputies of the corresponding levels) on income and property status. The income declarations of these individuals (as well as their children and spouses) are publicly available on the internet, covered in official media, and checked by control and supervisory authorities. Most executive authorities have established their own security services, whose purpose is to

---

55   Federal Law of December 25, 2008 No. 273-FZ "On Combating Corruption".

prevent the corrupt activities of employees of the executive authorities and their territorial bodies in the constituent entities of the Russian Federation.

No matter how actively the state tries to combat corruption, however, it cannot succeed in this battle without the help of ordinary citizens. Each and every Russian should and must live and work guided by the law. To avoid corruption, it is vital to understand one's rights, know how to protect them, and have a strong moral position which refutes the use of corrupt methods in private, public and professional life.

Citing data from the judicial department of the Supreme Court, the RBC reports that over the past several years the number of people convicted of accepting large bribes in Russia has grown at a record pace. In 2019, nearly 5,300 people were convicted of corruption in Russia. Of these, 1,247 received a bribe (+16.8% compared to 2018), and 1,595 people attempted to transfer illegal payments (+15.3% compared to 2018). The number of commercial bribes (226 sentences, +8.7% from last year) and mediation in bribery (226 sentences, +29.9% from last year) has also increased.

The Supreme Court also noted that the number of people convicted of 'petty bribery' (article 291.2 of the Criminal Code of the Russian Federation) has declined dramatically, however. In 2019, an amount of no more than 10,000 roubles was offered and accepted 31.5% less often than in 2018. According to RBC experts, most of these were drivers trying to buy off fines for traffic violations.

One of the most well-known researchers in the field of corruption is Ichak Adizes, founder of the Adizes Institute Worldwide (California), business consultant to several hundred companies, including the Bank of America, Coca-Cola, IBM, and political consultant to the governments of Sweden, Brazil, Israel and Mexico. He is a research consultant for the Executive MBA and MBA programmes at the RANEPA Institute of Business and Business Administration, and the author of 20 books on management published in 26 languages. One of the highest paid consultants in the world, his attitude to the problem of corruption is as follows: 'I have given lectures in more than 50 countries around the world, and almost everywhere there is the same problem — corruption. Why is this phenomenon so widespread and why is it not becoming less significant no matter how we fight it? There is a Jewish saying: "a hole in the wall invites a thief." At present, the world is undergoing rapid changes — the economy, people's lives, and technology are changing faster than ever before. Because of such rapid changes, a country's government can begin to come apart at the seams, and many holes appear in the wall. Corruption helps to find back roads and workarounds where the state system simply does not work. That's why it's impossible to deal with this phenomenon through severe punishments, such as executions, for instance, as in China. If you stop corruption, everything will cease to function. The thing is, corruption is the flip side of bureaucracy: if you need to pick apples in Mexico, the state will set 88 rules to regulate this apple picking. To work in such conditions, people will have to break the law, like it or not. That's why I advised the Mexican president to simplify regulation in all areas of business, to make it clearer and more transparent. Azides' recommendations seem to have resonated with the Russian government as well. In 2019, they began talking about a 'regulatory guillotine.'

Bureaucracy

Although the term 'bureaucracy' appeared only at the beginning of the XVIII century, the concept of such an administrative system has existed since ancient times. Its appearance was made possible by the invention of writing. Thus, we find the first bureaucracies as early as in Ancient Sumer and Ancient Egypt. In Ancient China, Confucius created a complex bureaucratic system. After the collapse of the Roman Empire, the Byzantine Empire built an especially complex bureaucratic system.

In one way or another, bureaucracy has been organising state activities since ancient times, and it becomes a problem when outdated rules, which no longer correspond to the spirit of the time, start to hinder the development of society.

In the view of the Russian researcher, Mikhail Kulapov, Russia's main problem is not bad roads (recall N. V. Gogol), but the chronic bureaucratisation of management. Not only does this lead to the consistent reproduction of negative results (sometimes including decisions that contradict common sense), it also hinders the ability to learn from the historical lessons of social development.[56]

It is becoming increasingly evident that Russian bureaucracy has significantly changed over the past fifteen years of reforms, expanding its influence on the country's life and mastering a variety of tools to protect and promote its interests in the new economic and political conditions. What hasn't changed much, or if it has, then for the worse, is society's negative attitude towards bureaucracy.

Whenever there is a need for change in the country, issues of bureaucracy involving its inefficiency and corruption come to the forefront. Such was the case twenty years ago when Mikhail Gorbachev launched perestroika and Boris Yeltsin continued his political activity under the same conditions. Meanwhile, the need to limit the omnipotence of the bureaucratic apparatus is traditionally combined in Russia with the demand for a strong state, justice and order.

Although most Russians do not equate bureaucracy with the state, they nonetheless recognise the importance of the bureaucracy as a kind of social glue designed to hold the state together. In a study, the majority of

---

56   M. Kulapov, P. Sergeev, I. Kokorev. Hereditary Diseases of Russian Bureaucracy and the Problems of World Development. // Economic Bulletin of the Economics Section of the Russian Academy of Sciences, 2014, No. 1.

respondents (67.5%) recognised that the country should be governed by experienced and qualified specialists, a view shared by ordinary citizens and government officials alike. The idea of public self-government appealed to only a third of the respondents (32.1%). A significant number of Russians (53.9%) believe that it would be a good idea to clean up the official apparatus, but there are many others, particularly among government officials, who have serious reservations regarding this matter (44.6 and 65.4%, respectively).[57]

The term 'regulatory guillotine' was proposed by the Jacobs, Cordova & Associates International Consulting Company, which developed the concept, and is actively used in the world.

It is a tool for the large-scale review and cancellation of regulatory legal acts which negatively affect the overall business climate and regulatory environment. The goal of a regulatory guillotine is a complete review of mandatory requirements undertaken with the broad participation of business and expert communities. The guillotine aims to create a new system of clear and concise requirements for business entities in the sphere of regulation, to remove excessive administrative burdens on business entities and reduce the risk of causing harm to protected assets.

In Russia, the time for such changes is long overdue.

In 2019, the Russian government declared its readiness to dramatically reduce the number of laws hindering business — the prime minister (at that time, Dmitry Medvedev) announced that the tool used to make an economic breakthrough would be a regulatory guillotine. The prime minister's order came after the government submitted a draft control and supervision code, providing for the creation of a mechanism to oversee a large-scale review of existing regulations. The authorities pointed out that another goal of this is to improve the system of business supervision,

---

[57] Bureaucracy and power in the new Russia: positions of the population and expert assessments. Analytical report. Prepared in cooperation with the Representative Office of the Friedrich Ebert Foundation in the Russian Federation. Moscow. 2005.

as many rules in this sphere have been in place since the Soviet era. The Ministry of Justice is going to invalidate more than 20,000 legal acts adopted in the USSR and the RSFSR between 1917 and 1991, as reported by TASS with reference to the press service of the Ministry of Justice.[58]

It's definitely high time. 'Specific outdated norms must be eliminated, and, in effect, a new legislative and regulatory framework must be created so that there are no unnecessary obstacles,' announced Andrey Nazarov, co-chair of Business Russia. 'It seems to me that the government is ripe for radical measures to improve the situation in this area.'

Preparing a road map for the guillotine has been entrusted to government apparatus, but it is not government officials or the Ministry of Economic Development that should identify excessive business requirements. The deregulation commission must become a new structure accountable to the prime minister, in the opinion of D. Tsygankov, one of the main authors of the CSR report on regulatory policy in Russia. Excesses can be identified by think tanks and specialised universities, he believes.[59]

---

58 URL: https://www.rbc.ru/politics/16/09/2019/5d7f54e69a79473f89f81e4b
59 Rbc.ru. Economics, January 15, 2019.

NEPOTISM AS A PERSONNEL POLICY

*Famusov: ... foreign employees are a rare thing for me.
More and more sisters, some in-laws,
and others from the family tree...*

A. Griboyedov, *Woe from Wit*

To arrange a cosy and well-paid job for someone's relative is the best way to express gratitude for a service. In Russia this is an immutable law, but not just in Russia, globally, hence the term 'nepotism' in English. The word is Italian in origin, dating back to the early Renaissance, when to strengthen their power popes allocated the highest ecclesiastical positions to their relatives. First in line were the nephews (Nepotismus, from ital. nepote — 'nephew' — A. K.), then sons and other relatives. Thus, entire papal dynasties came into existence — the Orsini, the Medici, the Borgia, etc. Only in the XVIII century, at the edict of Pope Innocent XII, could there be only one 'nepot' in the Cardinal's College.

Today, the word 'nepotism' is used to denote in a very general sense 'care and concern for a relative.' During the entire period the Russian state has been in existence, only in the time of Stalin was nepotism severely punished. Stalin was merciless: he imprisoned the wives of Molotov and Kaganovich, and Khrushchev's eldest son. Nor did he particularly favour his own sons, repeatedly removing Vasily, a lieutenant general, from office, and refusing to exchange Yakov, who was taken prisoner during the war, for a field marshal. Many of the wives, brothers, sisters and children of the Soviet nomenclature were, if not executed, then imprisoned.

Those days have passed, though, and no matter how much the West tries to spook us with the ghost of Stalinism returning, this is nonsense, and flourishing nepotism stands as proof. Moreover, the practice of appointing relatives to government positions has once again formed the basis of our state system.

In the era of Brezhnev, the principle of nepotism — 'strangers do not walk here' — played a leading role in creating the highest echelons of state and Party power. Yuri Andropov[60] tried to put an end to nepotism, but to no avail, and it was in part thanks to nepotism that the Soviet system collapsed.

In the 1990s, President Yeltsin and his 'family' turned over a new page in the history of nepotism. Yeltsin set the tone, and soon many 'nepos' of various ranks appeared in government circles. In principle, nepotism reflects the natural human desire to ensure the well-being of one's friends and relatives. Since we don't have an aristocracy, inheritance involves not a title but an equivalent social position and status. At one time, a top-ranking Party worker would ensure a 'position abroad' for his son; today it is a high-ranking position in a bank, company or a political party. Therefore, all the "juicy" government positions are occupied either through patronage, or they are bought. Just take a look if there are many on the Federation Council who actually come from the regions and republics they represent.

In modern politics, nepotism reigns supreme in all countries regardless of their level of development. In highly developed countries, narrow circles of oligarchs have to turn to relatives to preserve this capital, and along with it, their power.

Although nepotism can be seen as quite a natural deep-rooted phenomenon, however, the leaders of the state must understand that such preferential practices pose a serious danger to development in Russia. As an acquaintance of mine bitterly stated: 'I graduated with honours from the Academy of the Ministry of Internal Affairs and was at the top of my class. So what? From among us, only those with "connections" were given a "hand" to a position of power. But not one, NOT ONE of

---

[60] Yuri Vladimirovich Andropov — Soviet statesman and politician, head of the USSR from 1982–1984.

my friends — brilliant and enthusiastic young men, got anywhere near power.'

Disillusionment, lack of prospects for career growth, and the futility of noble motives to serve one's homeland lead either to apathy or the realisation that the way up the ladder is through the "money bag," so this must be acquired by hook or by crook. As a rule, lack of competition and objective selection from the talent pool results in rampant corruption and decay of the entire social system.

One can't help but recall the words of Confucius: 'There is good government when those who are near are happy, and when those who are far away desire to come.' Confucius and his successors founded a whole system of education for civil servants: officials were selected not because they came from a rich and noble family, but based on personal merit and intelligence, which was regularly tested in exams.

This is precisely why education remains to this day a huge incentive for the Chinese in attaining their ambitions. To this day, the temple of Confucius preserves the thousand-year-old stone steles with the names of those who successfully passed the imperial examinations for the title of official. In our day, the names of Chinese civil servants are not engraved on stone steles, but this doesn't make their lives any easier: more than 15 years ago, exams for officials were reinstated in China in order to fight corruption and nepotism. True, this doesn't eliminate corruption, but it does give people from 'far away' a chance.

It seems that the wisdom of the great Chinese philosopher has resonated with the Presidential Administration of the Russian Federation. In 2020, 541 people made it into the semi-finals of the Leaders of Russia competition organised by the Presidential Administration, according to the competition press service report released on April 15th. The first stage, including online testing of the participants in social studies and assessment of their 'leadership potential' had 8676 participants. Top score was obtained by 511 people, whilst another 30 demonstrated results in the top 75%.

There were many more men who made it into the semi-finals of the competition than women — 79.7% against 20.3%. The majority of participants who made it into the semi-finals were under 40 years of age (67.7%), and they came from 75 regions of Russian, among which Moscow (28.2%), the Moscow region (6.7%) and Saint Petersburg (5.9%) were dominant. According to Aleksey Komissarov, the head of the competition, the face-to-face stages of the competition will be held after the epidemiological situation in Russia is brought under control. The semi-finals include control testing and group tasks.

'The organisers want to demonstrate… that the keys to career mobility lie in their hands,' the expert stated; 'this is always vital in the sphere of staffing. They also want to show there is a new style in personnel policy, which is more modern and effective.'

'The President has set the task of making social mobility transparent, and platform has been created — Russia, the Land of Opportunities — an autonomous non-profit organisation which combines fifteen projects which anyone can try their hand at,' V. Davankov, Deputy General Director of the project stated. 'The number of such projects will grow. Undoubtedly, the state greatly needs a mechanism for social mobility. This year, we plan to launch at least twelve [federal] initiatives.'

The contest winners can participate in state Duma elections or become members of the Federation Council. Based on its results, seventy to eighty people will be selected, who will be trained by twelve mentors at the RANEPA Higher School of Public Administration, including deputies and senators. As Komissarov remarked, the organisers cannot guarantee that the winners will get to the Duma, but they will certainly be in demand in the upcoming elections.

Statements from senior government officials indicate that the problem is now a top priority:

THE RUSSIAN MENTALITY

'Mechanisms for social mobility should be aimed at making people believe the authorities are sincere in their desire to implement this, and this is why the process must be systematic. The worst thing is when 90% of people are not ready to use the social elevator. This is an area we need to focus on.' — Pavel Sorokin, Deputy Minister of Energy of the Russian Federation.

'For social mobility mechanisms to work, the system must be ready to lay people off, and lay them off not for promotion purposes or horizontally, as is often the practice. This is considered the norm for the system in a normal healthy society.' — Pavel Sorokin, Deputy Minister of Energy of the Russian Federation.

'Sberbank is developing at an impressive rate due to the development of its people. This is a conscious strategy, and we understand that every employee should be given a chance. More than 70% of internal appointments at Sberbank take place from the inside.' — Valeriya Zabolotna, rector, ANO DPO Sberbank Corporate University.

'We use all possible sources. Intelligent and capable personnel are as vital as oxygen to us, provided that we have our own mechanisms — base universities, etc. — but we are not ready to give up other opportunities. "Is talent everyone, or is it a select group of people?" That dilemma is long behind us. With us, it is each and every person. Our goal is to help people discover these opportunities.' — Yulia Uzhakina, General Director, ANO Corporate Academy of Rosatom.

In Russia, it is vital to pursue a systematic policy aimed at increasing the share of capital in the structure of national wealth, namely:

building the capacity of a university education;

improving the quality of the Russian vocational education system;

improving the soft skills of students — collective problem-solving skills, communication skills and creativity.

In terms of improving the level of medical care, which directly affects the quality of human capital:

increasing the role of primary healthcare, including the diagnosis, prevention and management of illnesses, instead of expensive treatment needed at later stages;

developing efficiency and increasing funding for healthcare through the implementation of treatment protocols based on the principles of evidence-based medicine and quality control systems; optimisation of redundant infrastructure and increased use of information technologies.

In addition to investing in education and healthcare, it is important to create a normal competitive economy at all levels so there is proper motivation (including decent pay in medicine and the education system), and for the social elevators to work. This will motivate people to acquire new knowledge and skills, to master technologies and, accordingly, be more competitive.

The underdevelopment of civil society

The English philosopher, John Bernal has observed that it is much more difficult to see a problem than to find its solution. To see a key problem, one mind, albeit even a brilliant one, is not enough. He believed that to understand a problem, the collective mind was needed, whereas to find a solution for it, all you need is skill.

A state can become stable and viable only when it relies on civil society and has its support and participation. In this regard, we can say that an urgent task for Russia today involves creating an effective management system, the goal of which is to increase the responsibility of the authorities to society. Therefore, the participation of Russian civil society not only in discussing, but also in effectively influencing the decision-making processes of the authorities, would help to solve the key problems of the state.

The Russian state needs to expand and strengthen its dialogue with civil society. Nevertheless, we must also take into account that civil society is still very weak, and it must be addressed on an equal footing rather than commanded from above. After all, a strong civil society is a positive response to the question of whether or not Russia should be a modern developed country. By definition, however, such a state cannot exist if society does not nurture free people.[61]

Russia's wealth lies not only in its natural resources, but also in its human talent — we have a unique cultural heritage and huge scientific and technical potential. Possessing such wealth, we owe all the citizens of our great country a decent life.

Sociological surveys indicate that Russian citizens today are particularly concerned about social injustice, inequality and poverty. Whilst inequality is a global problem, Russia is in third place among eighty-two countries on regional inequality, is in the top three on inequality of regions within the country among the states of Europe and Central Asia, and among the world leaders on inequality of wealth distribution. More than half of our citizens have no savings.[62]

The task of civil society structures in the context of a mutually responsible partnership is to prevent and, if necessary, oppose the bureaucracy. With regard to public control, appropriate expertise is necessary. Its intended purpose is to assess the regulatory impact of normative acts and the actions of authorities at all levels.

Without the active involvement of civil society and ordinary people, it is impossible to improve life in the country in any significant way. We often hear that citizens lack sufficient competence to participate in the discussion and control of management decisions. Some sociologists stress that public discussion of injustice and inequality issues is dangerous; supposedly, it could encourage an explosion of populism which would hinder the implementation of reforms. As if there were a certain "elite" that knows what reforms to implement, whilst the citizens do not.

---

61   Sidorenko G. I. The Development of Civil Society in Modern Russia: Trends and Problems of Interaction with the State / G. I. Sidorenko. — Text : direct // Young Scientist. — 2015. — No. 8 (88).

62   Report on the state of civil society in the Russian Federation for 2018. — M.: Public chamber of the Russian Federation, 2018.

Such an approach is fundamentally flawed, however. After all, the ultimate goal of transformation is a decent life for humanity. The decisions taken affect people directly, both in a positive and a negative sense; they experience the consequences first hand, not simply in theory.

The task of the elite is to take the true values and aspirations of the people, and use them to formulate pragmatic operational goals and objectives in such a way that the whole of society understands and accepts these goals and objectives. A consolidation around development goals thus takes place, society becomes united, and the state becomes strong.

Trust develops primarily through the participation of citizens in the development, implementation and control of decisions which directly affect their quality of life and the future of their children. A perfect example of what not to do was the pension reform, which was prepared in a traditionally bureaucratic manner and then presented to the population as a done deal. It's hardly surprising that people reacted negatively: according to opinion polls, citizens do not believe in increasing pensions after the reform and view all the changes as an attempt on the part of the state to force older people to work longer and take away their well-deserved pensions. Obviously, such a public atmosphere, in turn, contributes to the growth of distrust.

For the "Russian breakthrough" to succeed, a new quality of interaction between the state and society is essential: a mutually responsible partnership, an important aspect of which is a mass public initiative. We need a creative search for new unconventional solutions and the promotion of civic initiatives which would allow us to achieve the ambitious goals of national projects. Only civil society can push the bureaucracy to make decisions which reflect the interests of ordinary people and then exercise public control over the implementation of the decisions taken.

Only through dialogue with citizens can the state win the confidence of all groups and layers of Russian society, convincing them that it hears and understands their requests and is ready to respond. Therefore, any large-scale reforms must be based primarily on the interests and values of the citizens, and, it is on this basis that the strategic goals and objectives for the development and consolidation of society should be formulated.

At this point, it is impossible to say that Russia has developed a clear and working system of public control which at least partially corresponds to the Soviet system of public control. Among the main shortcomings are a poor awareness on the part of citizens about the opportunities and subjects of public control, a lack of coordination of the activities of public inspectors within regional and local authorities, the secrecy of data required for checks (in particular, in the sphere of environmental control), and, finally, a lack of sufficient powers for public inspectors and effective liability rules for ignoring the results of public control.

The question of expanding the scope of public control remains open. In particular, civil activists have repeatedly called for legislative consolidation of the ability to exercise public control not only over the activities of government bodies and other bodies and organisations with separate public powers, but also over economic entities: utilities, major banks, railway and air carriers, etc. However, representatives of the Ministry of Internal Affairs, the General Prosecutor's Office and the Investigative Committee who participated in discussing this issue in the Public Chamber of the Russian Federation are strongly opposed, maintaining this would lead to an overlap of the powers of state governing bodies whose responsibilities include the implementation of state and municipal control with the subjects of public control.

An important institution of civil society is the mass media, whose task it is to cover issues of public concern. In today's conditions, the media is gradually losing this social role. There are several reasons for this, but one of the main ones is the general crisis in traditional media, which is losing out to social networks in the fight for an audience. Under such circumstances, the media are forced to adapt to the current conditions and cover the so-called hot issues and scandals, whilst paying virtually no attention to high-quality investigations and social topics. It's a well-known fact that negative news is an easier sell, and the media today find themselves in a situation where they are trying to earn a buck on practically everything.

In his blog a few years ago, the Russian director, Andrey Konchalovsky wrote: 'Our government now presents the classic example of misunderstanding the problem. Police reform, the fight against corruption, Skolkovo, modernisation, nanotechnology — that is, the government is probably sincerely trying to modernise our state, but it fails to understand that economic reforms - which are certainly important - are not the most pressing issue. They reformed the police, changed its name, certified some folks here and there, and removed some others… But has anything really changed? Of course not, because Russian police officers and officials still have exactly the same values in their heads. The government can't understand that no modernisation will be successful if the Russian mentality isn't modernised, because that's where it all begins — in the mentality. Peter the Great, Stolypin, Trotsky and Lenin all tried to change the Russian mentality — with varying degrees of sincerity, but they could not; they failed, or perhaps did not have enough tools, which the state now has.'

CONCLUSION

Two years ago, the Valdai Club[63] released a report entitled "Life in a crumbling world," in which it suggested that multilateral cooperation is being curtailed. The crisis of international institutions is leading to anarchy, when each state will rely on itself to deal with the challenges of survival.

The events of 2020 are a stark confirmation of this hypothesis. COVID-19 is a temporary phenomenon, like all pandemics. However, it has catalysed processes which have been brewing for a long time.[64]

The ideals of integration and globalisation, which have already been shaken in recent years, are facing a new test of strength. No sooner had news of Brexit disappeared from the headlines than it became clear that in the fight against the coronavirus, as well as in saving the European economy, it's once again every man for himself. And that's not to mention the closed borders all around the world. Many ruptured chains of economic ties will not be restored — states will encourage an increase in the share of local full-cycle production.

The sovereign state turned out to be the only institution capable of acting in a sufficiently organised and effective manner. The illusion that the state can simply disappear from global politics, giving way to some entity that exists outside boundaries — political or cultural — has finally dissipated.

The state is also beginning to play a greater role in the economy — in the dispute between public and market interests the scales are shifting towards the former. Resistance to non-economic shocks, which is provided by the state and not by the market, is becoming a crucial economic

---

[63] The "Valdai" International Discussion Club is an expert and analytical centre, established in 2004 in Veliky Novgorod. The club owes its name to the venue of the first conference, which was held near lake Valdai.

[64] URL: https://ru.valdaiclub.com/about/experts/3750/.

indicator. After all, at a time when the economy has become truly global, politics remains subjective.

The usual ideological schemes lose their significance — first and foremost, the old dilemma juxtaposing democracy and authoritarianism. The crisis has shown that the viability and success of states is determined by a different frame of reference; one which is more related to culture, traditions and cultural mentality than to a country's political system. One of the main categories of the coming period will be ethical pluralism — the absence of any "correct" set of values that everyone must follow.

No matter how the situation with the global economy plays out after the pandemic, one thing is certain — the resource surplus will be replaced by its shortage. A fierce fight for these is inevitable. In the most extreme negative scenario, politics will be characterised by international Darwinism, the most archaic version of international relations.

New forms of state responsibility will be needed to mitigate the threats that arise from the difference in the balance of forces of those vying for resources that are in short supply. Regardless of how the international environment is structured — or if it loses its structure altogether — states will be left with the question of survival. It is essential to develop a system of adequate responses to the behaviour, interests and values of others.

The idea of relativity of sovereignty, which was brought forth by the liberal order in the early stages of its acquisition of hegemony, has already transformed into the idea of absolute power, which, on the whole, is natural.

The established world order is being replaced by a democracy of independent states, which dictates new requirements for responsible behaviour. The world to come must be much more democratic than its predecessor, and at the same time much more demanding of those making decisions. This is precisely why it presents such a wealth of opportunities for humanity to mature as a society of independent individuals — states.

What political conditions must be created so that this period of transformation of the world order can help competing value systems understand each other? The first condition is obvious: it is recognition by all players that others have the right to be guided by their own values. For many countries, such recognition is difficult. Second: to understand the values of others, education is necessary — a process of learning about them, political and cultural understanding. Recognition of pluralism provides for the appearance of 'values curiosity,' a sincere desire to understand others. Third, and most important, the competition of value systems must make way for their convergence. After this, common values may once again appear, the advantages of which have already been mentioned; the sole difference being that, in this case, they will be shared by everyone, and not perceived as imposed from the outside.

The current pandemic — manmade or not — is a crisis that is being used by the world's players to resolve certain issues and pursue their objectives. Under the cover of force majeure circumstances, not only has the global economy been deliberately steered into recession, but a whole new economic reality has been created. A fundamental restructuring of the entire system of economic ties and relations is taking place.

A key feature of the present period is the restructuring of the global economy. We can assume that in the current situation, the destruction of the existing world order of liberal globalisation in the interests of the United States will be accompanied by the formation of a new economic world order, the development of which will occur in the competition of integration structures with their centres in China and India, whilst maintaining the significant influence of the EU, the United States, and, hopefully, the European-Asian Economic Community.[65]

The emerging new economic world order may take one of several possible forms. The first one has already taken shape in China. It is

---

65   Report of academician S. Yu. Glazyev. Access mode: URL: https://karaulovlife.ru/news/zaklyuchitelnaya-chast-doklada-akademika-s-yu-glazeva/10415.

characterised by a combination of state planning institutions and market self-organisation, state control over the main parameters of economic reproduction and free enterprise, the ideology of the common good and private initiative, and demonstrates a tremendous efficiency in managing economic development. This has been clearly demonstrated by the impressively high development rates of the advanced industrial sectors over the past three decades, and has been reaffirmed by the effectiveness of the fight against the pandemic.

The second type of integral economic world order is being formed in India, which is the largest real functioning democracy in the world. The foundations of the Indian version of the integral system were laid by Mahatma Gandhi and Jawaharlal Nehru on the basis of Indian culture. Well-chosen priorities stimulated the development of key areas for the formation of a new technological order, and today India ranks first in the world in terms of economic growth.

The third type of new economic world order can be discerned in the mirage of the mass psychosis of the growing pandemic. From the depths of the deep state of the United States, voices can be heard demanding that a new world order be formed. In the wake of the pandemic, institutions are being created, claiming to govern humanity. In other words, the third type of the new economic world order implies the formation of a world government under the leadership of the American ruling elite in the interests of financial capital, which controls the issues of world currency, transnational banks and corporations, and the global financial market. This continues the liberal globalisation trend, supplementing it with authoritarian control technologies over the residents of countries deprived of national sovereignty.

Each of the varieties of the new economic world order described above involves the use of advanced information technologies, which are a key factor in the new technological order. All of them use big data processing methods and artificial intelligence systems, which are necessary for managing not only automated production processes but also people in the systems of economic regulation and social behaviour. The goals of this regulation are dictated by the ruling elite. The way each particular ruling elite is formed determines the essential characteristics of each of these varieties of the new economic world order.

The new world order will be formed in a competition between these three varieties of the new economic world order. That said, the third one excludes the first two which are able to coexist peacefully.

Undoubtedly, all the options for the development of the world community will face the following challenges of the new technological order:

The mass unemployment of those previously engaged in routine labour, which will be replaced by automatic control systems in both material production and services. These people will either need to be retrained for new creative professions, or given the opportunity of early retirement.

The split of society into a creative class of people engaged in creative self-realisation and a layer of society making do with service-industry jobs and the role of consumers. For these two social groups to coexist in harmony, working social elevators and social security systems must be in place, enabling the poor to receive a good education and ensuring a decent standard of living for those without knowledge.

Fragmentation of society by social networks, differentiated by worldview, moral values and needs. The integration of these network communities by the state should be carried out by harmonising their interests in achieving the common goal of increasing public welfare.

The erosion of social groups based on a physical sense of solidarity, and the sociopathy of a growing part of the population that is locked in virtual space. These people need special conditions for survival and self-realisation, requiring appropriate mechanisms of social adaptation. Their integration into society will form a key challenge for national security.

An increase in the free time of the population due to people being released from labour-intensive fields of activity. To use it creatively, opportunities for creative self-realisation unrelated to work for consumption must be developed. Beyond the threshold of this challenge, the possibility of a bright future beckons.

It seems that the world has entered a new period of instability, and this involves a challenge for Russia. Fyodor Lukyanov, editor-in-chief of *Russia in Global Politics*, believes that, 'Given Russia's extremely insignificant role in global economic processes… no military or political achievements can compensate for this. Clearly, there will be no miracle, and Russia will not become China, but a certain build-up of economic opportunities would make it possible to adjust the picture somewhat. Russia's problem is that we are portrayed as a dying monster, and many in the West perceive us in precisely this way. If you are indeed a real monster, then sooner or later they may want to start negotiating with you, to avoid possible confrontations. But if they think you're a monster now, and in five years your economy, demographics, and so on will inevitably lead to degradation, then it is easier to wait until such a freak dies of its own accord. Therefore, it would, of course, do us good to tone down the "monstrous" image, but it is even more important to show that this monster isn't going away. Thus far, Russia has been claiming a role that significantly overreaches its current economic capabilities. Ensuring a sharp growth of the country's economy is the only way for it to remain in the game. Because if it acts like an economic power of the level at which it is actually located, it will have to take an insignificant role in the world.'[66]

Thus, the task of significantly expanding the country's economy becomes not only a matter of internal concern related to improving the well-being of Russian citizens, but also an external factor, enabling us to

---

66   March 15, 2018, Source: Medusa, from the series "Russia — 2018"

take a worthy and stable position in the world.

Whether or not the state will take advantage of all the advantages of the Russian mentality, which has repeatedly demonstrated its ability to function effectively in uncertain conditions, depends on Russian society, including, to a large extent, on the country's leadership.

It is essential to free society's creative forces from bureaucratic fetters by eliminating outdated legal norms and to help business, at least for a few years, by easing the tax burden, enabling it to recover from the present crisis; to radically expand the opportunities for a new generation of leaders to enter all spheres of management, including high offices, on the basis of real competition and appropriate training; to encourage by all possible means the formation of an active civil society and use its potential for an equal dialogue with the authorities to enhance management decisions for the benefit of the effective development of the Russian state.

Such measures are currently under discussion and are being implemented in a somewhat hesitant manner, but the Russian economy needs a transformation on a different scale to take a qualitative leap forward.

SELECTED BIBLIOGRAPHY

Berdyaev N. The Fate of Russia. — M.: EKSMO-PRESS., Kharkiv: Folio. 1999.
Bulgakov S. N. Selected Works / comp., auth. intro. art.: O. K. Ivantsov, PhD.; auth. comments. V. V. Sapov, D. S. Novoselov. — M.: ROSSPEN, 2010.
Ilyin I. A. The World Politics of Russian Sovereigns // Professor I. A. Ilyin. Our tasks. Articles 1948–1954. Volume I. — Paris: Publication of the Russian General Military Union, 1956.
Ilyin I. A. On the Coming Russia: Selected Articles / Ed. by N. P. Poltoratsky. — M.: Voenizdat, 1993.
Klyuchevsky V. O. The Course of Russian History in 5 parts. — St. Petersburg, 1904–1922.
Lossky N. O. The Conditions of Absolute Good. — M., 1991.
Tyutchev F. I. Letters to Moscow publicists. I. S. and A. F. Aksakov. 1861–1872. 27. A. F. Aksakova. Petersburg. Wednesday, 20 September [1867] // Literary Heritage. Vol. 97. Fyodor Ivanovich Tyutchev. Book one. — M., 1988.
Shafarevich I. R. Essays in three volumes. Vol. 2. — M.: Phoenix, 1994.
G. Kodzhaspirova, A. Kodzhaspirov, Pedagogical Dictionary — M.: "Academy" Publishing Centre, 2001.
URL: http://chtooznachaet.ru/mentalitet.html.
Lyubchak V. P. Specifics of the Russian Mentality in the Context of Peacekeeping Issues. GOU VPO "Tomsk State University", 2010.
Yadov V. A. Regarding the National Specificity of the Modernisation of Russian Society. IS RAS, 2009.
V. A. Yadov, Clement K. et al. The Impact of Western Sociocultural Models on Social Practices in Russia. IS RAS, 2009.
Russian Society and the Challenges of the Time / ed. by M. Gorshkov and V. Petukhova. — M.: Ves Mir, 2017.
Lapin. Sociocultural Factors of Russian Stagnation and Modernisation // New Ideas in Sociology / Resp. ed. J. T. Toshchenko. — M.: UNITY-DANA, 2013.
World Health Organisation: Global Status Report on Alcohol and Health. 2018.
Lichutin V. V. Reflections on the Russian People. — M.: Institute of Russian Civilisation, 2013.

THE RUSSIAN MENTALITY

Artemova V. G., Filippova Ya. V. The Mentality of the Russian People: Traditions and Evolution. Nizhny Novgorod State University named after N. I. Lobachevsky. 2008.
Schubart W. Europe and the Soul of the East / Social Sciences and Modernity. — M., — 1992, — No. 6; — 1993, — No. 1–4; prev. G. Böll — 1995— No. 4, 1995.
The Anarchist Within: Clinical Reflections on Russian Character and Leadership Style, Manfred F. R. Kets de Vries, Human Relations. 2001.
Prokhorov A. Russian Model of Management. — M.: Publishing House of Art. Lebedev Studio, 2011.
Richard Pipes: Russia Under the Old Regime. — M.: Zakharov, 2012.
O. Chumicheva. The Project "Arzamas. The History of Russian Culture. Muscovite Rus". 2018. Lecture 6.
Federal Law of December 25, 2008 No. 273-FZ "On Combating Corruption".
M. Kulapov, P. Sergeev, I. Kokorev. Hereditary Diseases of Russian Bureaucracy and Problems of World Development // Economic Bulletin of the Economics section of the Russian Academy of Sciences — 2014. — No. 1.
Bureaucracy and power in the new Russia: positions of the population and expert assessments. Analytical report. Prepared in cooperation with the Representative Office of the Friedrich Ebert Foundation in the Russian Federation. Moscow. 2005.
URL: https://www.rbc.ru/politics/16/09/2019/5d7f54e69a79 473f89f81e4b
Rbc.ru Economics, January 15, 2019.
Sidorenko G. I. The Development of Civil Society in Modern Russia: Trends and Problems of Interaction with the State / G. I. Sidorenko. — Text: direct // Young Scientist. — 2015. — No. 8 (88).
Report on the state of civil society in the Russian Federation for 2018. — M.: Public Chamber of the Russian Federation, 2018.
Report of the "Valdai club", 2020. Access mode: URL: https://ru.valdaiclub.com/about/experts/3750/.
Report of academician S. Yu. Glazyev. Access mode: URL: https://karaulovlife.ru/news/zaklyuchitelnaya-chast-dokladaakademika-s-yu-glazeva/10415.
March 15, 2018, from the series "Russia—2018" Source: Medusa

REVIEW

V. V. Kozlov: The Russian Mentality as a Fundamental Factor in Russian Management Methods, Moscow 2020

History throws a long shadow. At the dawn of World War II Winston Churchill famously said that the Soviet Union is *'a riddle, wrapped in a mystery, inside an enigma'*. Churchill perfectly grasped how little understanding Europe west of the Polish-Soviet border had of Russia, a land that was beyond the pale for most politicians and scholars alike, let alone for the layman. It can be argued that the order of things changed precious little over the past eighty years – if anything, the Cold War merely added to the curious amalgam of ignorance and prejudices harboured by much of the world regarding Russia and events during the past thirty years did not do much to dispel them. Yet it would be a mistake to claim that debates about Russia and her peoples are confined to outside of her boundaries. On the contrary, since the reign of Peter the Great there has been a vehement debate in Russia over her nature; to what extent is it European? Or is it Asian? As Russia faced different challenges over the centuries the answers varied greatly, but the lingering uncertainty never disappeared: as if by forcing Russia down the path of Westernization Peter the Great let the genie of identity crisis loose and putting it back into the bottle has been impossible ever since. As the Venetian polymath Francesco Algarotti wrote in 1739 Peter the Great's new capital was meant to be a *'a window onto Europe'*, a testament to Russia's rise and embracing of European culture. As the philosopher Alexander Herzen noted, St Petersburg *'differs from all the other European towns by being like them all'*. But while Peter the Great promoted Western technology and culture, he rejected its liberalism. Behind the grand neo-classical façades of his new capital lay the sweat and blood of the 540,000 serfs and Swedish prisoners of war who toiled in the swampy marshlands during the first 18 years of construction, and tens of thousands of whom perished in the process. The political philosopher Nikolay Berdiaev, who believed that much of Russia's troubles stemmed from the *'inconsistency of the Russian spirit'*, described Russia's problem of straddling East and West as *'eternal'*. Despite his assumption to the contrary, however, the question of Russia's soul was largely a product of the 18th-19th centuries, for in earlier centuries Russians bothered little with the questions of existing between East and West. In other words, the great schism between 'European' and 'Asian' in Russia is a quintessentially modern product. Gallingly for Russia, even the simplest matters, such as determining where Russia and Europe ends and Asia begins was far from being an unproblematic issue, but a mostly bogus one. John Roberts' remark *'Europeans have long been unsure about where Europe 'ends' in the east. In the west and to the south, the sea provides a splendid marker ... but to the east the plains roll on and on and the horizon is awfully remote'*.

Such a rather long exposé dwelling on Russia's position between east and west in a review of a book dedicated to Russian mentality and the ways it bears on management might strike as something of an oddity but as V. Kozlov notes in the hard-hitting introduction of his admirable work, to understand Russian mentality one has to *'look back over our history and trace the process of the formation of national character'*. It is no surprise, therefore, that while focusing on the present, again and again Kozlov looks for examples from the past to explore the development of certain phenomenon to their fullest. He notes that *'an important feature of the Russian mentality is dreaminess. (…) exacerbated by poverty, has led to collective fantasies and dreams of universal justice, wellbeing, beauty and goodness. In general, Russians have tended to live in their dreams of the future. They imagined that the harsh and dull reality of everyday life* was merely a bump on the road to another life where everything would be different and where they would find reason, true happiness and joy. The whole meaning of life was in this imagined future, whereas the present counted for nothing.' Undeniably, chapter titles like '*Freedom of the Press*', '*Russophobia and nationalophobia*', '*Corruption*' or '*The underdevelopment of civil society*' leave little doubt that no stretch of the imagination could paint a picture of the Russian Federation being free of problems. On the contrary, as is the case with most countries across the globe, Russia faces a myriad of issues, prominently featured among them those of economic nature and such realizations provided the initial impetus for V. Kozlov to begin working on '*The Russian Mentality*'. As he writes, '*economy needs a transformation on a different scale to take a qualitative leap forward*'. Indeed, the very goal of his book is to throw light on issues not only related to how do the peculiarities of the Russian mindset translate to work ethic, for example, but also to what extent are structural reforms needed to create an environment where businesses can thrive. The goal is undoubtedly most commendable, and one can only hope that for all ebbs and flows, some conclusions of this book of outstanding learning will not only be utilized by those at the country's helm but also by those who, day by day, work and shape its economy, and its future.

Gerald Mako
Cambridge Central Asia Forum
Jesus College, Cambridge University

REVIEW

"The Russian Mentality as a Fundamental Factor in Russian Management Methods" by V. V. Kozlov. Edition 2.

When first asked to review "The Russian mentality as a fundamental factor in Russian management methods" by V. V. Kozlov, I at first thought this could be a bit difficult, expecting the book not to be in the best english and somewhat academic in scope and style. However, for an english speaker and reader, the book was surprisingly easy and enjoyable to read. As a westerner with long term experience and interest in Russia, it was also very interesting, particularly where some of the book's points coincided with my own insights into Russian mentality, but also where it explained factors that maybe I didn't previously understand.

The book lays out what Russian mentality means with foundations on what defines mentality, how Russian mentality is described by mainly Russian writers and experts, but also foreign writers, how Russian mentality is defined from the west, how Russian mentality has been shaped by events - both international and domestic - and particularly through several critical events over the last 100 years, how cultural & legal factors play a role, and how this feeds into Russian mentality with regard to Russian management. Russian attitudes to freedom of the press are discussed, particular in comparison to western attitudes to freedom of the press. Russophobia is discussed, both by Russians abroad and from the West along with challenges to Russian economic performance particularly with reference to corruption, nepotism, and bureaucracy.

Though I am not so sure that a recognizable continuity in Russian mentality survived firstly the Russian revolution, I have personally witnessed the continuation of a Russian mentality through the collapse of the Soviet Union. Though Kozlov throws doubt on this, I can see a continuation of the concept of Russia as a third Rome and in particular this updated influence on today's Kremlin. Russian messianism is alive and well and a not insignificant player in the recovery of Russia's military recovery since the collapse of the Soviet Union and Moscow's inheritance of the Orthodox mantle after the fall of Constantinople.

Several aspects of the Russian mentality are covered, particularly the historical preference for paternal despotism and centralised power. Further the Russian mentality preference for unquestioned loyalty to the state with the understanding that the state will provide for its citizens. Of course, this deal fell apart when the Soviet Union collapsed, but part of the reason for so much support for Putin is that he rebuilt that deal while stabilising and strengthening the Russian administration and recovering the economy. This is compared for the west's reliance on rule of law in entrenching individual rights and in particular private property rights. Kozlov has made several good points regarding the difference in Russian vs Western beliefs regarding the law, where in the West the law is regarded as almost unquestionable, whereas Russians believe in justice more than the law. Russians tend to have a week sense of personal rights, certainly when compared to the West and in particular the US.

I was once approached by a Muscovite policeman asking for what might be considered in the West a bribe. He mentioned several traffic laws that I might have broken. When I protested that these laws were contradictory and couldn't possibly relate to me, the policeman opined that there were indeed many laws in Russia, which is why they could be flexibly applied while at the same time being 'optional'. It was quite entertaining to hear this opinion on Russian laws from a burly Muscovite policeman, who had clearly put some thought into the merits of Russian legal system.

Closely related to Russia's mentality with regard to the law is Russia's attitude to Freedom of the Press. Kozlov mentions that though the West is sure that Russia has no Freedom of the Press, in fact there are some good reasons to believe this is not as true as it might first appear. For

THE RUSSIAN MENTALITY

example, he mentions how difficult it is to criticise anything related to Western Wars or Patriotism. Even the best journalists in the West have lost their jobs when questioning the reasoning behind western military action. Also, the author mentions how Freedom of the Press can be taken too far in the West, at least in the eyes of Russians. For example, insults against Mohammad or the Catholic Church would be considered unacceptable in Russia. There is little stopping criticism of Russian leadership at street level in Russia, though printed criticism is another matter.

Russophobia, both from Russians and the West is discussed by the author and its history going back to the 18th century. Anti-Russian sentiment has been a constant theme through the last 100 years of Russia's history and clearly continues to this present day, assuming it hasn't actually grown. Often, attitudes in the West consider Russia 'too big to continue', with plenty of support in the west for breaking Russia up both culturally and politically.

Of particular interest to me was the discussion of the three very different Russian civilisations that have existed in the last 100 years - Tsarist, Soviet, and post-Soviet. Each brought different attitudes and changes in mentality while also keeping some continuation of character. I often joke that the Russian character is no dissimilar to the Scottish character. Both tend to be dour and ostensibly humourless until you get to know them individually, when they become great friends.

As the author notes, relationships mean far more to a Russian than to a Westerner, which has indeed been my experience with my relationships in Russia. This is not really so true in the West. In fact, as compliance requirements grow in Western Companies, strong relationships are almost frowned upon. I have often witnessed a foreign company enter Russia believing that its world class product or service means sure success, only to find that without a good relationship in country, world class status does not mean as much as they might suppose. In fact, pride in world class status while not developing local relationships, can appear quite arrogant to the Russian mentality.

Items that I thought might be strengthened in the book are binding some of the previous discussion about mentality into the section on management, particular with regard to Soviet and pre-Soviet mentality. The author discusses some of the modern obstacles to modern Russian management in corruption, nepotism, and bureaucracy, but quite rightly also points out recent measures that have been taken to restrain corruption and reduce bureaucracy. It would have been interesting to hear to what extent these were factors in Tsarist Russia, though Stalin's efforts to stamp out corruption are indeed mentioned. The author mentions that despite the weaknesses inherent in Russia's management mentality, administration, and despotic leadership, nevertheless Russia progress through the last 100 years has been extremely significant with quite a number of globally significant successes, not least being their space program, their military capability, and their civil and military nuclear capability. It would have been interesting to hear more about how the Russian state overcame some of their inherent mentality-based issues to achieve such globally leading successes.

Also, it would have been interesting to hear more about Russian management and Russian mentality and a little less about the Russian economy and civil society, but maybe that's just my preference. It was however interesting to hear the authors opinion that though western governments tend to be administrators of competition - where competition was encouraged between and within sectors of the economy, Russia tended toward competition between administrations. I have often seen this in my business relations in Russia, where one administration might compete with another regarding an economic opportunity. In the West, the emphasis would be far more on the competitive advantage of the company related to the opportunity. This has often resulted in major misunderstandings between Western competitive companies and Russian administrations.

One aspect contributing to Russian mentality that the author mentions almost as a surprise, is the rise of the academic class. The 'flight

THE RUSSIAN MENTALITY

of the professors' under the communists and particularly under Stalin makes the rise of a significant academic sector all the more surprising. However, I have no doubt that the academic families of the Soviet Union were critical the successes of the Soviet Union and often formed the backbone of progressive and moderating behaviour in the Soviet Union. I have noticed that many of the children of such academic, and the officer class of the Soviet military too, have very similar attitudes and values in life to myself, being the child of an RAF officer during the cold war. This is one of the most surprising things about the Russian mentality that I have found myself.

One of the last factors that the author mentions with regard to Russian mentality and international relations is the importance of building a strong economy in an increasingly globalised world. Personally, I am not always fully supportive of some aspects of globalisation, but I fully agree with the author's point. It is important to become a serious economic participant in an increasingly global world if Russia wishes to stabilise its role and place in the world.

In summary, I found the book very interesting and surprisingly easy to read. The use of english flows easily, which is impressive given that the authors first language would appear to be Russian. I would recommend this book to anyone interested in the Russian mind and in particular Russian attitudes to business and the business legal and cultural environment.

Bruce Gaston,
Writer & CIS expert

REVIEW

"Having turned over the last page of Dr. V.V.Kozlov's book The Russian Mentality as a Fundamental Factor in Russian Management Methods, I can say without a shadow of doubt, that it is an impressive, all encompassing piece of academic research and a very entertaining read at the same time.

It is coherently structured around the concept of Russian mentality, exploring historical, cultural and geographical factors of its formation and manifestation at different levels of interpersonal communication.

The book could be useful not just for a narrow circle of specialised readers, but anyone who comes across the Russian model of interaction in business, social or family life.

The author approaches the subject from different angles analysing work of classic Russian writers and Russian thinkers who escaped the Soviet regime by emigrating abroad, and also opinions of foreigners working in managerial roles in modern Russia.

At times, when commenting on differences in Russian and Western European mentalities, Dr. Kozlov seems rather categorical and non-compromising. However, the readers must remember that it is simply impossible to present all the nuances of such an immense subject within the scope of one book. It is an invitation to polemic if you like.

To me, this research is not an attempt to dissect the famous Russian soul to understand its "mechanics" in order to utilise its powers for superior performance in international business. I can see its purpose in making the reader aware of the multi-layered complexity of a national character concept in general, supported by instances of its contextual representation.

Only time will tell if the overall globalisation and business internationalisation will erase those distinctive national traits, or will just create a temporary surface level dent leaving the colourful mosaics of the world's mentalities untouched. I personally hope for the latter."

Natallia Thompson, Translator

THE RUSSIAN MENTALITY

www.ingramcontent.com/pod-product-compliance
Lightning Source LLC
Chambersburg PA
CBHW031323160426
43196CB00007B/634